T0375185

DOOLEY'S PUB

A COLLECTION OF EROTIC SHORT STORIES

ROGER C. ZOCORT, M.D.

authorHOUSE®

AuthorHouse™
1663 Liberty Drive
Bloomington, IN 47403
www.authorhouse.com
Phone: 1 (800) 839-8640

Published by AuthorHouse 09/10/2018

ISBN: 978-1-5462-5718-9 (sc)
ISBN: 978-1-5462-5719-6 (hc)
ISBN: 978-1-5462-5717-2 (e)

Library of Congress Control Number: 2018910159

Print information available on the last page.

This book is printed on acid-free paper.

CONTENTS

CAST OF CHARACTERS (IN ORDER OF APPEARANCE)

Shauna Stevens, junior partner, Moore, Wiggins, and Short law firm
Julie Barrett, junior partner, Moore, Wiggins, and Short law firm
Robert Markham, sales representative, GE, Atlanta, Georgia
Richard Watson, vice president, Union Bank of Portland
Renée Salva, sales manager, Express Advertisement Agency
James Rowe, junior partner, Moore, Wiggins, and Short law firm
Suzanne Rowe, wife of James Rowe, court reporter
Harvey Johns, MD, cardiologist, Los Angeles, California
John Dooley, proprietor and owner of Dooley's Irish Pub
Megan O'Reilly, wife of John Dooley, business manager of Dooley's
Nedra Wiggins, senior partner, Moore, Wiggins, and Short law firm
Kevin Furrer, MD, internal medicine physician, Portland, Maine
Larry Hansen, programmer with MBI Corporation, Portland, Maine
Ronnie Anderson, no listed occupation, part-time cook, hairdresser, etc.
Sherrill McKinney, bank teller, Union Bank of Portland
Cheryl Swanson, executive secretary, Union Bank of Portland
Mildred Bowers, RN, local hospital in Portland
Derek Patterson, chief of security, Trans-Atlantic Shipping, Portland Maine
Braden Jordan, IBM computer installation, 1970; IT freelance, 2016
Christina Collins, sales clerk, 1970; retired sales manager, 2016
Serena Parton, daughter of Christina Collins, paediatric oncologist
Spencer Thomas, investor and stockbroker
Colleen Brannon, realtor, Kelly Williams Realty Elite
Karl Kilgore Henderson, MD (KK), clinical psychiatrist
Sally Hammond, visitor to Portland

Patricia, girl on the airplane
Geoffrey Kuban, sports editor, local Portland newspaper
Katherine "Kat" Masters, Spartacus Challenge athlete, home day care operator
Jenny McKinney, legal secretary, Moore, Wiggins, and Short law firm
Roland Barker, sales manager, Portland Mercedes dealership

PROLOGUE

Portland, Maine, most recent population 66,318, was founded in 1786 as a fishing port. Almost one hundred years later, in November 1894, Ian Dooley arrived on a steamship from Ireland, having shared a cramped cabin for eighteen miserable days as they crossed the storm tossed North Atlantic. He swore upon his mother's grave that at the first sight of land, he would walk or swim to shore. He did not need to do either because the *Queen of Ireland* docked at Portland's waterfront and offloaded some of her cargo, including Ian Dooley.

Ian Dooley, twenty-three years old, was an Irish emigrant son of a drunken father and a mother who'd died before he had any remembrance of her. He sought a new life in the promised land of the United States of America. Ian was a talented carpenter and soon found work in this new city. His first big break occurred after being in Portland only six months. A young lawyer by the name of Ezra Higgins was building a new home, and after seeing some of Ian's work, he hired him to oversee the finishing of the interior of his new house.

Ian and Ezra became good friends during this period. They often discussed the need for a good bar and pub to serve the more upscale patrons of Portland. They formed a loose partnership, with Ezra contributing financial backing and a storefront shop in a three-storey building that he owned. It was Ian's task to convert this area into a functioning bar and pub, and then to operate it for the partnership.

Ian was a remarkable craftsman, and his first task was to construct a beautiful forty-foot wooden bar from ship salvage lumber. That bar is still the centrepiece of Dooley's Irish Pub today. Stools, tables, and chairs soon followed, and the first barrel of good Irish whiskey arrived by ship in June 1896. Ian soon took over part of the larger rear area of the building, which had originally been designed as a stable. He finished off the interior, added a wooden floor, and set up a brewery. He was soon producing a very good draft lager, and the brewery quickly occupied the entire back half of the building. The business flourished as predicted. More space was needed, and the bar was expanded to occupy the entire street front of the building. Dooley's Irish Pub was recognised as the place to gather after work. According to their original agreement, the partnership was set up as a survivorship. When Ezra Wiggins passed on, Ian inherited not only Dooley's but also the entire building.

Ian married a local girl, and a family soon followed. They set up housekeeping in the front two apartments just above the bar, connected by a stairway into the back of the bar. His youngest son, Samuel, was the one most interested in the family business and eventually inherited the business upon Ian's death in 1940. Samuel had only one son, John, born in 1962 and now the owner and proprietor of Dooley's. The big neon sign in the front window proclaims it's the oldest and best bar and pub in Portland.

CHAPTER 1

THE BEST EVER

Shauna was twenty-nine years old, single, and a junior staff lawyer with Moore, Wiggins, and Short, a fifteen-person law firm in Portland, Maine. She was a fiery redhead with a temperament to match. She'd never found a solid relationship with a man, although she had dated many and slept with a few. She'd been very busy with law school, and now she was trying to build up her practice by working twelve-hour days, including the weekends.

It was early Friday evening following a busy week of an intense deposition and research on a particularly difficult case. She was sitting at the bar by herself in Dooley's Pub just off the judicial square, a frequent watering hole for lawyers and their staff. Although it had been six months since she and Edward had parted ways, she couldn't see herself with any of her male coworkers, most of whom were typical assholes.

Charlie Johnson, a young (at least by her standards) prosecuting lawyer in the DA's office, slipped onto the stool next to her and tried to start a conversation. She knew he was in the throes of a failing marriage, and the last thing she wanted was any additional complexity in her life. Charlie soon gave up and moved down the bar to a more promising young paralegal, and Shauna went back to nursing her Guinness.

Her last relationship was with Dr. Edward Mason, a divorced paediatrician. It had lasted longer than most, just over six months. His practice, a demanding ex-wife, and Shauna's own erratic schedule had left very little free time for them. Compared to her previous lovers, he rated somewhat better, but not by much. Their most recent getaway had consisted of three days in Boston. As she recalled now, they had spent more time on their iPhones than in conversation with each other. Soon after they returned to Portland, he suggested that they take a break from each other, which was fine with her. Edward's idea of good sex was to turn off his iPhone for ten minutes. He was usually considerate enough to wait for her to be satisfied, but not always.

She continued to reminisce. Maybe her best friend in high school, Marie, was right when she'd said that Shauna was destined to be an old-maid lawyer. One of the senior partners in the firm, Nedra Wiggins, was fifty-five years old and bragged that she was a professional virgin, whatever that meant. In high school, Shauna and her girlfriends had shared stories of romantic encounters, mostly fantasised, but some were real. Marie in particular seemed to be the expert and told her that if Shauna didn't do it before she graduated from high school, there was definitely something wrong with her.

In the fall of her senior year, the opportunity finally presented itself. Jack was seventeen years old, good-looking, a star on the basketball team, a real hunk, and definitely prime meat. When Jack asked her to go on a date with him, Shauna promptly agreed—and then consulted Marie for advice. From what she had heard (and Marie confirmed it), he would want to go all the way on the first date. If she did not agree, then that would be their last date. She remembered thinking at the time, *OK, the time is right—now or maybe never.*

As predicted, they saw a movie, went to the local drive-in for hamburgers and fries, and then headed to the far back corner of the local Walmart parking lot. The entire experience from the first kiss to zipping up his pants took six and a half minutes. She thought, *Is that all that there is to sex? People die for this, get divorced, have affairs, and start wars over it? Really?* Aside from being generally uncomfortable, there was no pleasure or satisfaction associated with the encounter. Once was enough with Jack. Shauna made a mental note: *No more athletes. They are crude, self-centred, and insensitive.* Later, these criteria of selection extended to a much larger population of professions.

In college she had joined a sorority, hoping to improve her social life. However, she met with the same dismal results. Boys and men seemed to have only one thing in mind, and it was not satisfying their partners. One encounter still stood out in her memory as unique.

Henry was a math major and a real computer whiz, and on top of that, he was not a bad-looking guy. He was likable, he seemed to have plenty of money, and he was surprisingly sociable considering his major. They had spent a number of evenings together at the library working on particularly difficult (for her) math homework, and they truly seemed to enjoy each other's company. He never dated anyone, and he never made any sort of move towards her. Looking back on it, she had definitely pressured him into asking her out. After five dates with no overt moves on his part, Henry had become a challenge, and she decided to take the initiative.

They were in the front seat of his beautifully restored '67 Chevy Bel Air, parked in the lot behind the men's dormitory. After some preliminary kissing, she casually brushed the front of his pants as a test to measure his response. Henry immediately froze in total panic, but he made no move to escape or object. They engaged in some more closed-mouth kissing. In retrospect, she should have realised by this time that this was not going to work. He made a clumsy attempt at squeezing her breasts, and she made another pass by the front of his pants, recognising a substantial erection. *So far, so good*, she thought. While he was concentrating on her breasts, she unzipped his pants and pulled out his erect organ.

To her amazement, and to Henry's complete mortification, he had an instant ejaculation, spraying her, himself, and the dashboard. In total panic, he leapt out of the car, making an attempt at assembling himself as he ran into the dorm. All this excitement without saying a word to her.

Well, that didn't go too well either, she thought as she walked back to the sorority house. *I am more and more convinced that sex is grossly overrated.*

Henry never showed up for math class again, and it was rumoured that he'd dropped out and changed universities.

At the pub, Shauna ordered another Guinness, silently resigning herself to spinsterhood.

A few weeks later, she was working on a new case that was not particularly challenging but very time intensive. It was a child custody case with the father trying to get permanent custody of his twelve-year-old daughter because the mother had recently been arrested for prostitution and drug possession. The case was not difficult but created an enormous amount of paperwork. She was working this case with one of the other junior partners in the firm, Julie Barrett. They had split up the preliminary discovery, record review, and court appearances, which was a much more efficient use of their time. Julie was a thorough and compulsive investigator, which made working with her a pleasure.

Julie was thirty-four years old, and she had a trim figure with short, dark hair and a shy personality. In the course of their time together while working, they had spoken about failed love experiences on a number of occasions. Shauna learned that Julie had been married for three years to an abusive husband who was a local police detective she had met while working a mutual case. Fortunately, they had no children, but it still ended badly, with him frequently pleading for her to come back to him.

As the last case on a busy Friday afternoon docket, Judge Houston ruled in favour of the father, granting him full custody with no visitation rights for the mother, but with prejudice in case the mother made a dramatic recovery in her lifestyle, which was not likely.

It was late when they had carried all of their material from the courthouse back to the law firm, and Julie suggested they go to Dooley's Pub to celebrate and unwind. The place was always busy, but on Friday afternoon it was generally worse. Happy hour was from five until seven, and the pub was noisy and packed.

They found two seats at the bar, and after two drafts of Guinness, they began to relax. The conversation turned back to men, as it commonly did, and they were sizing up some of the new faces with comments that would not be considered politically correct. As usual, nothing came of their observations.

"How about one more round, and we call it an evening?" suggested Shauna.

"Let's do it one better," suggested Julie. "This place is so noisy that it's hard to think, much less have a conversation. Why don't we go to my apartment? It's just two blocks from here, and we can open a good bottle of wine and continue to drown our experiences, along with the men that caused the problems."

Julie laid her hand on Shauna's arm and let her fingers slowly slide down the back of her hand, pressing down lightly upon her fingers. She took Shauna's hand and helped her down off of the barstool.

Shauna felt a sensation that was totally foreign to her. She really liked the soft touch and quiet manner of Julie, and she felt an attraction to her that she could not catalogue into her past experiences. They walked out of the bar with Julie still holding her hand, and not only did Shauna not object, but she rather liked it.

Julie's condo was well appointed with tasteful artwork and modern furniture in the entryway and living area. It was the modern, open theme with furniture and low dividers demarcating the space between living, dining, and kitchen areas.

Julie opened the sliding door, covering a small but well-appointed wet bar with a fully stocked wine refrigerator. She selected a bottle of Cake Bread Cellars Sauvignon Blanc 2012. A few quick turns of the corkscrew, and two glasses were produced from the shelf and filled. She motioned to the white leather couch, and she and Shauna sat together and toasted some of the good and some of the worthless men in their lives.

Julie finally broached the question that both wanted answered but neither had asked. "Have you ever made love to a woman?"

A few years earlier, Shauna had been asked the same question and was so offended by the suggestion that she'd left without saying another word. This time it seemed different. Julie was not making the suggestion in a lewd or even misrepresentational fashion; it was an honest inquiry between two women who were obviously more attracted to each other than just as friends and coworkers.

"It really is very nice," Julie said. "Women understand what a woman wants and needs, whereas maybe one man in fifty has this understanding and the ability to make a woman feel fulfilled before, during, and after sex."

Shauna agreed. "A man's brain falls to the head of his dick, and after it's all over, the rest of his sense drains out, and he is done."

Julie laughed. "That pretty well sums up every one of my past experiences." Both women raised their glasses in a toast. They held each other's gaze for a long, extended moment.

Shauna had always felt uncomfortable looking anyone directly in the eyes for more than a few seconds. She often utilised focused and primary eye contact as an aggressive cross-examination tool, but never in a situation like this.

As she continued looking into Julie's face, she realised that she had never really looked at her that closely. Julie had a plain but beautiful face with full lips and a thin accent of eyebrows and eyeliner, but was almost devoid of any other type of makeup. She did not need it.

They continued holding each other's gaze, and then Julie moved slowly and deliberately towards Shauna. Their lips touched just briefly, and then she pulled back.

Shauna had never felt this level of arousal following such minimal contact with anyone. She reached up to Julie, placed her hand behind her head, and pulled her mouth back to hers. They melded in a long, deep, thrusting kiss.

They separated, and with no spoken words, Julie took Shauna's hand and led her to the bedroom.

The bedroom continued to reflect Julie's excellent taste in all things good. A king-size bed dominated the centre of the room. A small sofa was under the large picture window, with a clear view of downtown Portland forming a perfect backdrop. The remainder of the furniture was modern and precisely placed.

"It's been a very long day. If you want to freshen up a bit, I will go use the guest bath. You should find everything you need in here," Julie said as she motioned to the luxurious bathroom just off the bedroom.

Shauna stood in the glass and marble shower stall and let the warm water pulsate over her body. She could not help but think, *What am I doing? What am I thinking? What will other people think? Easy answer: I'm doing exactly what I want to do, and to hell with thinking about it or what other people care about.*

She stepped out of the shower, towelled off, and put on a blue silk robe that she found hanging behind the door. Then she stepped back into the bedroom.

Julie had already pulled down the duvet, revealing down pillows and silk sheets. She stood there in a matching blue robe with fresh glasses of wine in her hands. She toasted, "To tonight. Let tomorrow be what it may." They touched glasses, took a long sip of the wine, again locked gazes, and set down their glasses on the nightstand.

Julie shrugged the robe off of her shoulders and let it slide softly to the floor. She had a trim body with small, firm breasts and just a hint of well-trimmed black pubic hair.

Shauna followed Julie's lead, dropping her robe to the floor and revealing a buxom and very well-proportioned body, as well as a thick patch of golden pubic hair.

They stood for a long moment, taking in each other's features. Shauna had never really paid that much attention to other girls in the locker room or dormitory showers. This was totally different; each wanted the other to take in all the features of her body.

Shauna slowly embraced Julie and pulled her against her body. They pressed together, and their mouths met in a deep, passionate kiss. Shauna's hands played down the small of Julie's back and cupped each of her cheeks as she pressed her body firmly against Julie's pelvis. After a long moment, they slowly broke free and slipped into the bed, lying side by side.

Julie rose up on one elbow, held a steady gaze at Shauna's face, slowly smoothed back her luxurious hair, and let her fingertips play over her face, across her forehead, and over her neck. She slowly repeated the pattern of gently caressing her eyelids and skimming with the softness of a butterfly over her lips.

She covered each side of her neck, going back and forth with her fingertips gently skimming along the surface, each time moving farther down onto her bare chest and her breasts. Julie lightly kissed both of her closed eyes and gently brushed across her lips her tongue, probing deeper. Shauna opened her mouth, and their tongues passionately explored each other.

Julie continued advancing down her neck and throat, her lips and tongue lightly touching Shauna's skin. She reached her breasts, gently caressing and kissing her erect nipples.

Julie's touch was unbelievably soft and tender, pushing Shauna further into the intoxication of a level of pleasure that she had never experienced before. Julie tenderly cupped her breasts, gently sucking both of her nipples before moving down to the soft skin of her upper belly.

She moved slowly and deliberately back and forth over the soft white skin of Shauna's upper abdomen, kissing and caressing each part of it, but slowly and deliberately advancing down to her lower belly.

When Julie reached the upper limits of the line of soft hair across Shauna's pubis, she stopped advancing and moved slowly right and left across this boundary, gently kissing the soft skin and tantalising the upper limit of golden hair.

Shauna was wild with pleasure. This level of erotic excitement was beyond containing. She could feel the fullness and the heat as blood engorged her pelvis and wetness filled her femininity.

Go on down. She silently formed these thoughts. Shauna had passed the point of restraint and could no longer stand the anticipation of what was surely to come. She pushed Julie's head and face firmly into her pelvis. Julie had been waiting for this level of acceptance as Shauna willingly acquiesced.

Julie's face was buried in the soft wetness, and both women were at the peak of excitement. Shauna's vulvar lips were hot and swollen as Julie's tongue deftly found the crease between them and plunged deeply inside.

Shauna could no longer contain herself and pushed wildly upwards, but still with her hands on both sides of Julie's head, forcing her deep inside her. Julie tightened her legs together and without touching herself achieved a violent and prolonged orgasm driven solely by sensations created by the encounter. Shauna simultaneously reached a climax that was more intense than any she had ever experienced. She repeatedly pulsed over and over again until she was spent and relaxed.

Only then did she open her eyes and look down at Julie's face, registering the malevolent grin that was spreading across her lips.

"No!" screamed Shauna. "I couldn't stand that again."

It was to no avail as Julie buried her face one more time into Shauna's soft, wet pelvis, but this time her tongue had another target: Shauna's fully erect clitoris. Julie's tongue rapidly rhythmically moved back and forth across the taunt organ, eliciting sensations even more intense than what Shauna had just experienced. Julie, her legs tightened together, was pulsating in rhythm with Shauna. The orgasm started rapidly and expanded to a full explosion of pure ecstasy for both women, but that was still not enough for Julie.

"Enough, enough! I don't think my heart can stand this much longer!" Shauna cried, but Julie was unstoppable. She then began to rhythmically suck on the already expanded organ until Shauna was sure that it would rupture or she would die in total ecstasy.

The final procession of wave after wave of cascading orgasms enveloped both women until neither had the strength to continue, and they fell back into each other's arms, their bodies drenched in perspiration and slick with the heat of their encounter.

As the first rays of the sun began to trace across the window, they were still wrapped in each other's arms, totally exhausted but totally satisfied. They may never have an opportunity to get together again, but in reality they both knew that anything after that first night could never reach that level of intensity and satisfaction.

A few weeks later, Julie was promoted to partner and soon transferred to the Boston office. She moved out of Shauna's life, but never from her memory of the best ever for both of them.

Conclusion

Sexual attraction can occur just as strongly between same sexes as between opposite sexes. Sexual attraction to another person of the same sex remains a subject of countless stories since the earliest days of recorded documents. In other cultures and in previous times, sexual intimacy between same-sex partners has ranged from total prohibition to completely uninhibited. Generally most societies look upon this as a moral issue. The "modern" culture of today is relaxing these barriers from the social and religious artificial prohibitions that were in place thirty years ago.

This chapter illustrates the hesitancy that was felt by Shauna when initially approached by Julie. Once this psychic barrier is breached, the individuals are free to fully enjoy all of the pleasures that each one can bestow upon the other. Until each individual can fully reconcile this mental conflict within her own morality, then she will always doubt the wisdom of such a union. Shauna, as you will see illustrated in succeeding chapters, is able to come to terms with this conflict, and as a result she becomes a more free-spirited and open-minded individual.

Questions

1) How did Shauna's earlier experiences with men lead to her willingness to explore same-sex romance?

2) Do you agree with Julie's approach to introducing Shauna to a same-sex experience?
3) Does this story accurately illustrate the appeal of a gentle, caring sexual approach?
4) Would it surprise you to know that same-sex intimacy is a standard and acceptable part of many cultures, past and present?
5) As a woman, do you find it uncomfortable to think about or discuss having sexual relations with another woman?
6) Even if you are declared heterosexual, have you ever had feelings of sexual desire towards another woman?
7) Do you feel that woman-on-woman sexual intimacy is morally wrong, or can you accept it as a personal choice issue?

CHAPTER 2

THE AWAKENING

Wednesday had ended up like every other day that week, with cold rain, multiple trips to the courthouse, and a lot of paperwork. Shauna was seated on her favourite barstool in Dooley's Pub, nursing a Guinness. *You know you have a problem with your social life when you have your favourite barstool at the local pub,* she thought.

It had been almost five months since she and Julie had gone to her apartment that night. She'd seen Julie a few times at work and at Dooley's since that evening, but the subject of that late-night encounter never entered their conversation.

She and Julie never mentioned their intimate relationship directly, although Julie gave Shauna numerous openings to revive their relationship. They remained very good friends and were professional enough that this relationship never interfered with their ability to work together.

Julie had completed her move to Boston in February, and one of the best things to come from their friendship was Julie's apartment. Julie was trapped with three remaining years of a five-year lease on her apartment. Shauna had a one-month cancellation clause on three rooms that she was renting in an older house on Deering Street, which necessitated an uncomfortable walk to work, especially on a cold day. Shauna agreed to take over Julie's lease on her apartment, which was much nicer, fully furnished, and much closer to work and to Dooley's. Although it was over twice as much rent as she was currently paying, she rationalised, "What am I going to do with my money anyway? I work hard for it, so I may as well enjoy it. Besides, I don't even have a cat to leave it to."

Shauna never did feel right about being with another woman, although at the moment it had felt wonderful and awakened a force within her that she had never known before. She would always look at sex with a much different perspective after this, but she still preferred a male relationship—if she could find a suitable one. The law firm where she worked had no prospects, and Dooley's was for marriage dropouts looking for rebound. *I'm almost thirty years old and am destined to become an old maid just like Nedra,* she mused.

She hardly noticed the older gentleman who sat down next to her. He ordered a gin and tonic, and she continued to keep her attention directed to her Guinness. She couldn't help periodically glancing at his reflection in the bar mirror. He was well-dressed and clean-shaven, with a touch of silver in his dark hair. He had steel-rim glasses, and she guessed him to be at least twenty years older than she was. She immediately dismissed him as too old and noted a wedding ring; he was also too attached.

So much for another dead-end? How can it be a dead-end if it didn't even start?

She finished her second Guinness, and he never paid any attention to her, which was great with her. She paid the tab and left the bar to go home. "Maybe I need a cat after all. Every old maid has a cat. On second thought, cats are way too much trouble with no real payoff."

It was a typical early April night in Portland. The spring thaw and its accompanying cold rain had started yesterday and was expected to continue throughout the weekend. She walked home slowly in spite of the steady cold drizzle. She liked to turn her face up to the rain, she always did even as a little girl. Her mother would always warn her, "You will catch your death of cold," but it never happened. *A few colds, but I'm still alive. I like rain.* She walked on to her apartment.

The following evening, she was again at her barstool and was still on her first Guinness when he walked in and again occupied the stool next to her. He initially spotted her in the bar mirror and then turned to face her. "Well, we meet again."

"I didn't realise that we met in the first place," retorted Shauna in her usual leave-me-alone voice as she slipped off her barstool and headed to the ladies' room.

The bartender, Big John Dooley, grandson of Patrick Dooley, the original founder of the bar, broke the tension and asked the man if he wanted his usual gin and tonic.

A really good bartender, he thought. "You remembered me," the older gentleman said.

"Always try to," replied Big John.

"Sorry. I seem to have offended the young lady who was just here."

"No, that's just how she is. She is one tough lady lawyer. Never lets her guard down around strangers."

"By the way," the man said as he extended his hand, "my name is Robert Markham. I'm in town this week for a medical convention."

"Big John here," John said as he engulfed his hand. "Shauna is really a very sweet lady, just kind of touchy with strangers."

Shauna returned and found a fresh Guinness waiting for her. She glanced over at Robert and realised he was looking at her.

"Can I help you, or what?" she growled.

"Sorry I offended you. I really did not mean to. I saw you last night and thought you looked lonely and might want to talk to someone."

"As John has probably already told you, I don't mind being alone, and married men don't interest me at all."

Robert slowly and reverently rotated the ring on his left hand. "My wife passed away in March four years ago of cancer. And yes, I have a problem: I can't seem to let her go," he mumbled apologetically.

Shit. Did it again, thought Shauna. "No, I should be sorry for being so rude. When a single girl sits at a bar, she gets all sorts of unwanted advances, and I just lump all men into the same bucket. Most of them are assholes; some are just a little worse than the average."

"Well, I do not have any evil intentions. I'm in town through Saturday at a medical convention at the Hyatt. My name is Robert Markham, and I'm from Atlanta, Georgia."

"I am Shauna Stevens, and I am a junior attorney at Moore, Wiggins, and Short here in Portland. Are you a doctor? What kind?" Her last medical experience with Edward was still fresh in her mind.

"I'm not a doctor. I'm in sales. GE X-ray machines. I'm the southeastern regional sales manager for GE. I live in Atlanta, occasionally."

Shauna took in more of his features while he explained in more detail what he did for a living. *Very nice-looking, just enough gray hair, must be much older. I would bet at least fifty,* she thought. *Crap, he could be old enough to be my father.*

As the evening moved on, Shauna was surprised at how well and how easily she could talk with Robert on a wide variety of topics. He asked about her law practice and listened patiently to her rant about bad childcare and a poor judicial system that wouldn't go after deadbeat fathers.

"God, I am sorry. I'll bet that was a fifteen-minute testimony you probably did not want to hear."

"On the contrary. You presented a very good case, and if I was the judge, you would have won the verdict."

Shauna laughed and held his forearm for a few moments. Embarrassed, she pulled away. He acted as though he did not notice and proceeded to change the subject to the loss of X-ray film being replaced by digital radiographs. "Had to learn an entirely new science in just a few years."

"We've had the same changes. Everything is now digital, but for some reason law firms still use an unbelievable amount of paper."

The conversation lasted through her self-imposed limit of a third Guinness, and Shauna was ready to leave. Robert insisted on paying the bar tab—he was better than the last deadbeat lawyer friend she'd had a drink with.

Robert paid the bar tab with cash and followed her out of the bar. "Can I get you a cab or offer you a ride? I could drop you off on my way back to the Hyatt Hotel."

"No, thanks. I live just around the corner, and the cool air feels really good."

"It's raining," protested Robert.

"Don't mind the rain at all," she said as she turned and headed towards her apartment.

"Will you be here tomorrow?" Robert asked as she was leaving.

"I probably will," she said as she glanced back over her shoulder at him.

While walking back to her apartment, the cool mist in her face, she felt much better about herself than she had in a very long time. *That was really very good just to be able to talk to somebody other than another lawyer.*

The Friday evening crowd was heavier than usual when Shauna arrived at Dooley's. Her stool was occupied. Then she saw Robert farther down the bar motioning to her to come over. He was guarding an adjacent barstool.

"Thanks for holding a seat for me; the crowd is really heavy tonight. Good seeing you again."

"I was hoping you would be here this evening. I thought we had great conversations last night. There seems to be no subject that you don't have some knowledge about, and I would love to continue talking with you," replied Robert.

As Shauna sat down on the stool next to him, a Guinness magically appeared in front of her. Big John winked and moved on down the bar.

"I've known Big John for years, and now you're his new best buddy," quipped Shauna.

"I wouldn't know about that," said Robert with a most sincere look in his eye.

Shauna was an excellent interrogator, and after two more drinks, she knew every aspect of Robert's life story, but he knew much less about her. She liked it that way.

He grew up in Georgia and graduated from Emory with a master's in engineering. Then he went to work for GE as a service engineer. He found it very easy to work with people, eventually applied for a position in sales, and was now the district sales manager for the south-eastern part of the United States for GE diagnostic radiology. With thirty years on his resume, he could retire, but he loved his work. His kids were grown and gone, and he had no wife and no dog. With no real home responsibility, he didn't mind being on the road. So why stop working?

They had talked for over two hours without anything to eat other than bar snacks, and Shauna was again at her self-imposed limit of three Guinnesses. During this time, casual touching of arms and then hands, combined with good conversation, had put Shauna at total ease with Robert. He was kind and considerate, never rude or vulgar in his conversations. After such a short period of acquaintance, she found herself more attracted to him than any of the men she had dated over the past few years.

"They have really good fish and chips here, if you are hungry," she said. "Or, it's getting late, and this place is still pretty noisy. Would you like to stop by my apartment for a nightcap? I'll bet I could find some cheese and crackers, or even something more substantial if you are really hungry." She looked at him. This was the second time in six months that she had made intimate, prolonged eye contact with another person who was not being interrogated.

Surprisingly, Robert was hesitant. "I really don't want to obligate you or become overly involved. It's been four years since my loss, and quite some time before that, since I experienced any intimacy due to her illness. You are the first woman in years whom I have talked to non-professionally for longer than five minutes, and I feel like I've known you forever. Here I am babbling away. Honestly, sometimes I think I'm a real klutz around women."

Shauna held his hand while still looking in his face. She realised that he was slipping into a deep pool. She said, "Maybe we both are little hesitant and scared. It's been a few years since I had a male friend." *Good legal manoeuvre—never be specific.* "Don't worry, I won't bite—much. I also can't afford any sort of long-term commitment, but I don't want a one-night stand either. Does this make much sense to you?"

"Perfect sense," he said as he placed three twenty-dollar bills on the bar for Big John.

"We never did get one of those famous fish and chip platters you are extolling."

"Maybe next time. You'll love my cheese and crackers."

The rain had stopped, and the sweet smell of the salty air coming off of the bay and mixing with fresh rain was refreshing as they walked hand in hand the two blocks to her apartment.

She used her card key to get into the lobby of the apartment building, smiling and waving at the lone security guard who was sitting behind his desk and keeping an eye on all of the surveillance monitors. She knew there was also a TV back there that probably had the latest basketball game playing. He smiled and nodded but otherwise made no acknowledgement of her companion.

She summoned the elevator, selected the floor, and opened her apartment door.

"That's a lot of major security," remarked Robert as he removed his tie and carefully folded his coat over the back of a chair near the entryway.

"That's one of the features I really like about this building. I feel very secure here, and you noted the discretion of the security guard. It didn't look like he was paying any attention, but he knows everyone in this building, and he knows everyone who normally visits. He can be one mean son-of-a-bitch if you cross him. This is one of the most sought-after apartment-living properties in the downtown area."

Shauna walked over to the bar and slid open the door. "Make yourself at home and pour yourself a drink. In the wine refrigerator, I have a bottle of pinot that I opened last night. I'm going to take a quick shower and get more comfortable—business clothes are tolerable only so long. There is a guest bathroom off of the living area, if you need to freshen up or anything."

Shauna made a fast pass through the shower, grabbed a clean bra and panties, and put on her blue silk robe. *I know what I'm thinking, but what does he expect? What does he think of me? Was I too pushy, too bold, and too ready?* She went back into the living area to find Robert sitting on the couch and studiously perusing one of her coffee table books about Great American railroads with a gin and tonic in his hand and her glass of wine sitting beside him on the table.

She somewhat nervously sat down beside him and picked up her glass of wine. "Here's to tonight. Worry about tomorrow when tomorrow gets here." They touched glasses and briefly sipped their drinks. She then noticed a fresh slice of brie surrounded by Bremner crackers on a small silver plate in front of them. "Glad you found that. You really know your way around the kitchen, don't you?"

"I always liked to cook, and for the past few years, I have been fending for myself. When you are alone, you learn to cook and improvise. Half the time, though, I don't remember what's in the cupboard or the refrigerator, and I'm a terrible grocery shopper," answered Robert.

She cut off a small piece of brie and smoothed it onto a cracker, washing it down with a good swallow of wine. She leaned back against the cushions, fixing her gaze steadily on Robert as he nervously tried a bite of cheese and crackers, promptly breaking the fragile cracker in half; everything ended up on the rug.

"Sorry, I was trying to make a good impression and ended up making a mess," he said as he carefully picked up the pieces and folded them into a napkin.

"Don't worry about that. We have a great maid service here."

She reached over and placed her hand on his arm, letting her hand slide down to the back of his hand and ever so lightly dragging her nails along his skin.

He held both of her hands, and they drew closer together.

Shauna said, "I want no misgivings or misunderstanding about what we are doing or might be going to do. If you feel like you need to escape, now is the time to do it."

Robert moved closer. "I've been hiding under a rock much too long. Being with you for the past two evenings has been the first time I've felt alive in many years."

Shauna passed a light kiss across his lips and leaned back. Robert's hands moved to her shoulders and then to the back of her head, and he pulled her forward. Their lips touched ever so lightly, and then with more pressure. Neither was sure who opened one's mouth first, but their tongues were soon frantically searching each other in an intense embrace.

They pulled apart, and Robert released the sash on her robe and pushed it off her shoulders. Shauna began slowly working her way down the front of his shirt, unbuttoning one button at a time painfully slowly, sensually escalating with each move.

She pushed his shirt back and then deftly released the catch on her bra, throwing her arms forward, allowing it to slide to the floor, revealing the most perfect pair of breasts that Robert could remember. He gently caressed the backside of both his hands down the front of her chest, skimming lightly across her nipples.

They were caught up again in a powerful embrace. Their mouths locked together, and their tongues explored the deeper recesses of their dental work. Their hands were moving every place they could find. Shauna made a tentative pass across the front of his pants, determining that there was considerably more life and action here than she'd originally anticipated.

Shauna, now clad only in her bikini panties, pulled away first. She took his hand and led him into the bedroom. Shauna pulled back the duvet and stretched out on the bed.

Robert, caught in an awkward moment, wasn't quite sure what the next move should be. Shauna sensed his uneasiness, sat up on the edge of the bed, undid his belt, unzipped his pants, and let them fall to the floor. At this point, there was no concealing his erection, and so she pulled down his shorts, revealing a fully erect organ dripping with anticipation. Holding it carefully with one hand and cupping his testicles with the other, she gently pressed her mouth over the engorged head and then proceeding to swallow as much as she could accommodate.

Robert placed his hand gently on her shoulders and caressed her thick-spun copper hair as she methodically stroked away at his organ. Unaccustomed to this much attention, he rapidly approached climax, which he definitely did not want to do so soon.

"That is absolutely phenomenal, but you need your turn."

She released him, pulled her panties down, threw them into the corner, and stretched out on the bed. Robert freed himself of the remainder of his clothes and lay down beside her.

"Do you want to turn off the lights?" Asked Shauna.

"Unless you want to, I like to see what I'm doing," replied Robert, propping up on one elbow, admiring the perfect lines of her face, and lightly stroking her hair.

He alternated between slowly caressing her face and kissing her on the forehead, closed eyelids, and lips. He caressed down both sides of her neck, across her shoulders, and onto her breasts. This was followed by gentle kisses and the light touch on skin with his tongue.

With both of her arms around his neck, she locked him into a tight embrace, pressed herself against his body, rolled over on top of him, and kissed him long and deeply.

She pulled away and sat astraddle his waist, both arms pressed against his shoulders. Her long hair perfectly framed her face. Robert gently massaged both of her breasts.

She rose up, pushed down to his pelvis, and guided him smoothly into her. She was surprised at how unbelievably good this felt. Edward had never liked what he'd called the "aggressor position". She began rocking back and forth slowly at first, then with more of a rotating motion, forcing him deeper into her until Robert moved his hands down to her pelvis.

"About two more pushes like that, and I'm going to lose everything," he said.

"Can I just sit here and think about it for a few minutes, then?"

"Just don't move."

"Just a little bit?"

"Not even slowly."

This time Shauna closed her eyes and pushed firmly down on Robert. She leaned forward, tightened her pelvis, and experienced a single spiralling orgasm without moving at all. She held her position transfixed as the surge slowly subsided, and then she relaxed.

Shit, that was so fucking good I thought I was going to die, she thought.

Throughout all of that experience, Robert had managed to hold his composure by sheer willpower. When she finally opened her eyes, he was looking at her. "That was probably the most spectacular thing I've ever witnessed," he said. "How did you do that without moving?"

"I have no idea, but I would love to do it again," she said as she began slowly undulating her pelvis against him.

Robert again placed his hands firmly on her pelvis and then slowly lifted her off of him. "Let's try something else for a few minutes while I regain my composure."

He gently rolled her over on her back and began sliding his tongue lightly across her belly, working his way toward the golden line. He slipped around between her legs and gently buried his face into her soft pelvis. She was wet from the past encounter, and his tongue slipped easily between the lips of her labia.

A cry of pure ecstasy escaped from her as he thrust his tongue deeply into her wet vagina. She arched her back, grasped him with both hands around his head, and pushed him as far into her as he could go. It only took a few thrusts, and she reached another screaming climax, followed by another, another, and yet a fourth time until she pushed his head back. "My god, you're going to kill me, that feels so good."

Robert proceeded to slowly lick his tongue up and down both sides of her labia, flicking across her erect clitoris. "Stop, stop, stop! Give me a break." He didn't stop, and he was sure she really didn't want him to. He centred over the engorged organ and proceeded to suck as much of it as possible into his mouth while massaging it with his tongue.

Shauna bucked and screamed as she had climax after climax, and Robert persisted in his massaging. Finally, she grasped him by his shoulders and forcefully pushed him away, quickly switching positions and burying his organ deeply in her mouth while massaging his testicles.

"If you don't stop that you're going to get a mouthful," pleaded Robert.

It was too late to stop anything. Shauna buried him deep in her mouth as he pulsed repeatedly until he was spent. She looked at him and laughed. "Poor thing! I think we broke it."

"It's very good at self-healing," retorted Robert. She moved up his body, and after a long, full, mouth-and-tongue kiss, Robert said casually, "Tastes like somebody came in your mouth." Both of them broke up into hysterical laughter.

They were a sweaty, sticky pair, and after a few minutes of lying there together, they got up and took a shower together. After lots of body wash and suds, Robert quickly sprung back to life.

"That was truly a remarkable resurrection," said Shauna, understating the dramatic healing process that had just taken place.

They went back to bed, holding each other very closely, and promptly fell asleep.

Shauna looked at her bedside clock and saw it was 6.38 on Saturday morning. The side of the bed where Robert had been lying only a few hours before was cold and empty.

Just like a man. Get the job done and slip out in the middle of the night, she thought. Then she smelled the coffee.

Robert was at the centre island of the kitchen, working on a three-egg omelette with a cup of coffee in his free hand. He poured a cup of coffee and handed it to her. "I never knew a lawyer who didn't drink a lot of coffee. Hope you don't mind my taking over your kitchen?"

Shauna wrapped her arms around his waist and lay her head on his shoulder. "You can invade my kitchen anytime you want to."

"For a bachelorette, you have a well-stocked kitchen," remarked Robert.

"I love to cook. In a family of three girls and five boys growing up in central Oklahoma, you learn to cook."

"We have a few more hours till I have to be at the Hyatt to supervise breakdown of our exhibit area and check out. My plane to Atlanta leaves at seven tonight."

Shauna took another drink of coffee and looked at Robert. "Then a before-breakfast appetiser might be a good thing to do," she said as she pushed the eggs aside and embraced him in a long, deep kiss.

Later, as they sat at the kitchen bar finishing the omelette, Robert remarked, "I will be in Boston the first week of June. Do you think you could come up with a real good reason to be visiting there at that time?"

Shauna looked over the top of her coffee cup with a satisfied smile on her face. "Date, time, and place. I'm sure my calendar says I'm supposed to be in Boston."

Conclusion

In the first chapter, Julie was able to break down many of the social barriers that had plagued Shauna for many years. Here, Shauna learns that the pleasures of sexuality can be released and fully enjoyed once these barriers have been breached. Her previous unsatisfactory experiences with men would have made this amount of freedom with Robert almost impossible to achieve without her same-sex experience with Julie. Under that circumstance, she was not threatened by Julie and had no previous bad experiences to form artificial mental barriers.

Shauna learned that sexuality can be enjoyed to its fullest extent once the individual learns to bypass the stigmas and prohibitions that have been instilled over the years within our psyche. Because these barriers are derived from many sources, often they need to be individually broken one at a time.

The second obstacle that she and Robert needed to overcome was the significant differences in their ages. They were able to overcome this artificial boundary because love truly knows no age differential.

Questions

1) Did a satisfying same-sex episode change Shauna's basic sexual desires?
2) Compare the approach to intimacy made by Julie in chapter 1 with that of Robert in chapter 2.

3) How do you feel about Shauna taking the lead with Robert? Do you approve of the way she offered him a graceful way out if he didn't want to participate?
4) Did the age difference between Robert and Shauna affect their relationship?
5) Would the encounter between Robert and Shauna have been likely if it hadn't been for Shauna's experience with Julie?

CHAPTER 3

SURPRISE

Richard Watson, forty-five years old and recently divorced, was having by his definition "a blue funk day". As a vice president of the biggest bank in Portland, Richard had a good job and a good income, and he still had some money left in spite of a very significant divorce settlement. It had been a busy week at the bank with what seemed to be endless meaningless meetings, and most of this past afternoon had been spent dealing with a very testy client who felt that the bank was charging too much interest on a construction loan. *All of this, and no one to go home to. Maybe I need a dog. They say they are good babe magnets when you take it for a walk. I could sit here in my favourite booth in Dooley's, sipping Guinness all evening, and nobody would care. Not the imaginary dog, and probably not even me.*

He had seen her walk in earlier and sit down at the bar. Really nice figure, probably late twenties or early thirties, long auburn hair, and stylish clothes. He remembered seeing her here at Dooley's in the past, chatting with friends. She was apparently a regular. Tonight she was alone, as was he. *Interesting, but I've pretty well had my fill of women and the problems they bring,* he thought as he turned back to his draft.

He looked up over his glass and realised that she was looking at him. She slowly turned her gaze away and back to her drink.

OK, why the hell not? he thought as he slipped out of the booth and walked over to her.

She turned towards him and smiled, showing her beautiful face, perfect make-up, and sparkling teeth.

"Hi. I hope I'm not being forward, but I've seen you in here many times before, and you look like you've been stood up this evening," offered Richard.

"Not really stood up. It's just that I made no plans for this evening, and with no place better to go, Dooley's is always my first choice."

"Well, same problem, lousy week," replied Richard. "For lack of a better offer, would you care to join me at my table?"

"That would be great. I would love to have some company," she said as she slipped off of her barstool and extended her hand to him. "Renée Salva. I work at the downtown Portland McGraw Ad Agency, and we have had an absolute bitch of a week."

"Richard Watson. Same week—must be in the air." He took her hand in his and held it a little longer than a casual handshake.

They returned to his table, ordered another round of drinks, and proceeded to develop a loose acquaintance. This process was usually accomplished by credentialing people and places locally, thereby establishing some credibility of their identification. They each determined that the other was a well-established local person and no obvious threat. She was thirty-two years old and unsure of her ultimate direction in life, but she was very vague about previous relationships. He was never able to determine if she'd been married or involved in a long-term relationship—not that it really mattered. He, on the other hand, spilled his entire life story to her over the next two hours with little embellishment.

The conversation slowly became more intimate, involving more touching of arms and hands. It was now well after nine o'clock, and the bar was beginning to slow down as people drifted homeward with or without companions.

"Would you be concerned about my intentions or offended if I invited you back to my apartment for a nightcap?" inquired Renée.

"No on both counts. In fact, that would be very nice of you. I have really enjoyed the evening talking with you and had hoped we might be able to continue our relationship," replied Richard.

Richard paid the bar tab, and they walked hand in hand out the front door and onto Congress Street, Renée directing the way and heading towards her apartment.

They walked slowly back to Renée's apartment. Although it was mid-July, the night air was still brisk, and in spite of the city lights, they could still make out a myriad of stars.

She opened the door and escorted him into the foyer. He helped her off with her jacket and hung it in the coat closet, casually draping his jacket and tie over a nearby chair.

"If you want to freshen up a bit, you can use the guest bathroom. I need to take a quick shower and should be done in a few minutes. Take your time, and pour us two glasses of wine. The glasses are just above the wine refrigerator."

Richard found a nice Riesling in the refrigerator, uncorked it, and poured two glasses.

Renée came out of the bedroom dressed in a pink satin robe that was tied at the waist but very loose at the top. Her long auburn hair hung shoulder length, and she had exactly the right amount of make-up on her face.

He handed her one of the glasses, and they toasted to a continued interesting evening.

They shared a light, tentative kiss. With no resistance, Richard pursued the kiss a little more vigorously. His tongue flicked across her lips, she opened her mouth, and they slowly blended together. Her robe was open just enough to reveal the medial half of two perfect breasts with just enough showing to be tantalising.

Richard could not wait any longer. He placed his wine glass on a nearby table, pulled her to him, and kissed her deeply and long. Their tongues eagerly explored the depths of their mouths.

His hands held both of her breasts, and as he nudged the robe back off of her shoulders, it dropped to her waist, still held by the sash. He alternated kissing each breast.

He pulled the sash on her robe, and it fell to the floor, revealing an erect penis.

To say that Richard was surprised would definitely be an understatement.

"I hope you're not disappointed?" Renée said.

"Shocked is a better term. I had never even thought of you this way," stammered Richard. "I-I just don't know what to say or what to do."

"If you have never tried this, why not? You were enjoying me, and I was certainly enjoying you, up until a few moments ago, so nothing really has changed. I just think of myself as a girl with a big clitoris."

As she talked, she unzipped Richard's pants to find that he also had a very good erection in spite of the recent surprise.

Renée led him into the bedroom, stood at the foot of the bed, pressed her bare chest against him, and again kissed him long and deeply. Richard responded in spite of the ambivalence of the situation.

While standing there, she proceeded to slowly and methodically unbutton his shirt while caressing his chest. His shirt dropped to the floor, and she quickly unbuckled his pants. They also fell to the floor.

She knelt down in front of him, pulled his shorts down, and proceeded to take his erect and dripping organ into her mouth. Richard did not object. He cupped the back of her head as she methodically sucked and stroked him.

She pulled him down on to the bed beside her, moved smoothly over on top of him, and wrapped her arms around him, kissing him deeply while pressing her pelvis and erect organ beside his, both trapped between the walls of their abdomens.

She undulated rhythmically, pressing and rubbing their bellies together, the bare flesh surrounding both organs, which were now making the area slick with their own secretions. By now, Richard had lost all ambivalence and was fully committed to whatever they were going to do. Both she and Richard were breathing heavily, pressing and rubbing against each other.

Richard was the first to reach orgasm, almost immediately followed by Renée as they pressed violently against each other, mixing pools of semen between their bellies.

They laid together for a few more minutes gently kissing, and then Renée slipped down to the side of him and with her free hand explored the impressive results of their lovemaking now spread across Richard's lower abdomen. She leaned down and ran her lips and tongue across his abdomen, tasting the mixture of their fluids. Richard's spent organ was discarded to the side.

Her fingers were still slick with their combined secretions as she moved them across Richard's lips. He tentatively tasted her fingers and then eagerly sucked them into his mouth.

They continued lying side by side, saying nothing. Many unanswered questions ran through both of their minds.

Renée finally broke the silence. "I don't know about you, but that was absolutely awesome. I can't remember when coming felt so good."

"I have to say," replied Richard, "never in my wildest dreams would I have ever conceived a situation like we just experienced. I was always taught that lovemaking was between boys and girls, but this opens up a world of fascinating possibilities. You look and act like a girl, and you feel like a girl except for one large difference that I never before considered being an object of my interest."

Renée squirted a shot of Astroglide into her hand and began slowly massaging Richards's primary organ of interest. She softly and smoothly rubbed over his penis and down onto his scrotum, coaxing life back into the previously flaccid organ. "It feels better if you get everything really slick."

Richard hesitantly but purposefully began exploring her more precious parts, enjoying the sensation of massaging and stroking another person's penis. Soon they were both fully erect.

He continued his exploration by tentatively taking Renée's organ into his mouth and relishing the sweet flavour of the free-flowing, lubricating secretions. While firmly holding the base, he swallowed the full length of the organ as far as he could insert it into his mouth and throat, realising that Renée now had him fully erect and ready for anything.

"Are you ready for the next lesson?" she said, grinning at him.

"I think I know what you have in mind. I've come this far, so no turning back!"

Renée rolled onto her back, spread her legs, and slipped a small pillow under her pelvis. She placed one hand under her scrotum and pulled it up, and with the other hand she began massaging Astroglide into her anus. First one finger, then two as she stretched the reluctant orifice. Richard watched in fascination while continuing to slowly stroke himself.

She directed him, leaning forward on his knees and taking his erect organ. She skilfully guided it past her tight anal sphincter. Very slowly but with a steady pressure, she allowed him to enter until his head slipped past the constricting muscles, and his entire shaft then buried itself within her.

She let out a cry of pleasure as his erection pushed firmly against her prostate, releasing a flood of erotic sensations. But strangely enough, as the mechanism works, she lost her erection.

Richard slowly stroked in and out, repeatedly pushing against her pelvic organs and eliciting deep and intense pleasure with each movement, both for himself and Renée.

She continued to massage her semi-limp penis in rhythm to his stroking and had soon revived it into full stamina. Her stroking became more intense as Richard pushed harder against her until she reached another climax onto her belly wall.

She then backed Richard out of her. "This time I want you to come in my mouth." She rose up and took his organ's full depth into her throat, continuing to vigorously stroke the shaft until Richard could stand it no longer and filled her mouth.

They both fell back exhausted on the bed but continued to gently rub over each other's body.

"I'm not sure I want to give up women just yet," remarked Richard as he looked deeply into her face. "But this sure was a good start to a completely new way of considering sex."

Conclusion

Ours is not to judge anyone's sexual preference or to hold them in moral judgement because they don't agree with our vision of morality, religion, political correctness, or actual written legal statute. The breadth of sexuality has an extremely vague, grey interface between clearly male and clearly female. One pair of chromosomes determines the physical make-up, but there are a multitude of other genetic codes that determine sexual preference because it is influenced by heredity, genetics, and external influences.

Homosexuality and transgender personalities have been a staple of myth and stories from the beginning of recorded history. It is obvious that no amount of religion or legislation is going to ultimately persuade individuals who are perceived to be outside of the norm to change. They have learned to love, live, and adapt to a world of hostility and intolerance. For those of us who can appreciate people for what they are rather than what they look like, we can make a place for each of them in our society.

Renée is an example of a person who is totally divided within herself. She relates to herself as a female, yet she also retains a component and drive that is very much male. She does not truly display ambivalent sexism, but more gender indecision driven by the current circumstance.

Questions

1) Were you shocked at the surprise? Do you think Richard behaved appropriately?
2) This story is full of experiences that are unfamiliar to most people. Do you find any of them unacceptable? If so, are your objections because of your training in morality, religion, legality, or some other factor?
3) Transgender people are often considered less socially acceptable than even gay or lesbian individuals. Would you feel this way about Renée?
4) If you knew Renée as a person, would you consider her as the female that she presents herself to be or the male that you know that she is?

CHAPTER 4

THREE IS NOT A CROWD

James Glenn Rowe III was thirty-four years old and was, a junior partner at Moore, Wiggins, and Short in Portland. The week had been long and difficult with two depositions and counselling with two separate expert witnesses in this particularly complex case.

Clyde Jon was seventy-eight years old when he was involved in a car crash where he rear-ended a pickup truck with enough force to set off his airbags and slam his seatbelt into the pacemaker/defibrillator on his left upper chest wall. He was seen at a local Portland hospital emergency room and, after many hours of lab and X-ray evaluation, was cleared for discharge home. He had three broken ribs on the left side but no other injury and no evidence of pneumothorax. At no time during the emergency room evaluation was his pacemaker checked.

Two days later, he went into ventricular fibrillation at home. His wife administered CPR until the first responders arrived and took him to the hospital. During this emergency room visit, it was noted that the pacemaker failed to respond as a defibrillator and was thought to be malfunctioning, probably as a result of the trauma of being hit by the seatbelt. A pacemaker check done at that time, however, showed the unit was functioning normally and that the defibrillator function was turned off. Although Clyde recovered, he did suffer a stroke during the episode of ventricular fibrillation and was partially paralyzed on his left side, which necessitated his being moved from his home to an extended care facility.

His family was now suing the original hospital emergency room physician for failing to check the pacemaker, as well as the pacemaker manufacturer for a faulty unit. A full analysis of his pacemaker showed that it was still functioning correctly, but the defibrillator option had been turned off. Whether this was caused by trauma to the unit at the time of the crash, or whether it was turned off at some previous visit, was impossible to prove.

The expert witness for MEC, the pacemaker manufacturer, did an excellent job of presenting the technical facts related to the robustness of the pacemaker related to trauma. It was his contention—and he made his points quite well—that trauma alone could not have turned off the defibrillator setting, but that it must have been done at some previous visit, or perhaps it was never initially turned on.

The second deposition of the week was the first hospital emergency room physician, who had been covering the ER by himself for six hours prior to Clyde's arrival following his automobile accident. The doctor eventually admitted under interrogating pressure from the plaintiff's lawyer that he was more concerned with Clyde's broken ribs and possible pneumothorax than with the pacemaker, which appeared to be in place and functioning normally.

The second expert witness was Dr. Harvey Johns, a professor of cardiology at UCLA. He was considered to be one of the most authoritative national experts on pacemakers and cardiac devices. He testified that he had never witnessed a pacemaker spontaneously change its settings based on trauma unless the unit was very badly damaged or essentially destroyed. Dr. Johns further testified that even if the pacemaker had been checked at the time of that first visit, it would have been found to be functioning normally, but with the defibrillator function turned off, which was not that unusual. His only concern was that the emergency room physician should have checked with Clyde's cardiologist, or at least recommended that Clyde be seen within the next few days by his cardiologist or regular physician. The opposing counsel tried all of the usual manoeuvres of questioning, but Dr. Johns was unshakable in his opinion.

Dr. Johns had come into town Wednesday evening, and all day Thursday was spent preparing him for the deposition on Friday. He went through endless scenarios: what if they asked this type of question, and what would his answer be to that type of question. By the end of the day, both Dr. Johns and James felt like they needed a drink and a good dinner in order to just wind down from the stress of the week.

James texted his wife, Suzanne, asking if she would like to meet them for drinks at Dooley's, followed by dinner at their favourite seafood restaurant on the wharf. She had already wrapped up her last transcription and was getting ready to start home, so she was more than receptive to the idea.

They met in Dooley's for a short drink and then walked down to the waterfront for dinner. Dr. Johns, or Harvey as he insisted on being addressed, turned out to be a very outgoing and likable person—much different from the person James had initially anticipated. Although he was all business at the law firm, he was now totally relaxed and a much different person. They had a great time, and it was obvious that Harvey had a hard time keeping his eyes off Suzanne's chest, which had been enhanced by the best plastic surgeon in Boston. James always enjoyed it when other men admired Suzanne.

The evening turned out quite well, with all three of them becoming good friends and sharing many stories and experiences over dinner. After a short walk back up the hill to the Residence Inn, the Rowes said good night to Harvey and proceeded to walk on to their apartment.

"I really liked Harvey," expressed Suzanne. "Think he might want to play?"

For a number of years, she and James had experimented with mixed couple sex, sometimes with disastrous results, but most of the time the encounters were very satisfactory and a lot of fun. One of her close friends, Julie Barrett, who had previously worked at the same law firm as James, had participated in threesomes with them a number of times. James always got turned on by watching Suzanne and another girl engaging in oral sex. The level of stimulation always enhanced his performance, and even though Julie was more partial to girls, she certainly didn't mind participating with him while Suzanne watched. Suzanne always said that he was more fun when there was someone else involved to enhance the level of stimulation.

"I will obliquely approach him on this tomorrow and see what his general thoughts might be. He is a nice guy, and it could be good fun."

The deposition finally concluded about 4 p.m. on Friday, and people were eager to be on their way either to the bar or home. Earlier that morning over coffee, James had suggested to Harvey that he might come by their apartment and unwind from the week's work. Harvey was more than receptive to the idea. With a midmorning flight on Saturday, it would be good to relax that evening.

"Are we still on for this evening?" inquired Harvey.

"We certainly are. I just texted Suzanne, and she is already home for the evening and will put together a snack. We will have a few drinks and see how the evening goes," replied James.

See how the evening goes? thought Harvey. *I know how I would like for it to go. I sure would like to get my hands on Suzanne's chest. Maybe I could do it under the pretext of a physician's breast exam. Ha!* "That sounds great," he said. "I will stop by the hotel and change clothes. If you give me the address of your apartment, I will meet you there at the designated time."

"Suzanne suggested 6.30," replied James.

"Very good. See you then."

Harvey arrived at their door promptly at 6.30 and was met by Suzanne, now dressed in a white sweater that buttoned down the front. She was obviously not wearing a bra and was more than pleased with her clothing choice, noticing the fact that Harvey had a hard time looking at her straight in the face. *This could turn out to be a fun evening,* she thought.

James prepared their drinks, and soon they were seated on a large, overstuffed couch in front of a low marble coffee table. Suzanne set a tray of hors d'oeuvres in front of them, and they proceeded to make small talk, mainly related to how the depositions went and whether James thought that this case would finally go to trial. Suzanne was sitting beside Harvey, and she continued to openly flirt with him, which he appeared to be finding somewhat awkward.

James looked at them and smiled. "Don't worry. She likes you, and I certainly don't mind if you don't. I always enjoy it when other men take notice of Suzanne."

"Well, James, it is very difficult not to notice Suzanne. A beautiful face, a gorgeous figure, and a dynamite personality. What more could you want?"

"And she is really superb in bed," quipped James, garnering a playful slap on the arm from Suzanne.

James could feel his erection growing while watching Suzanne and picturing Harvey with her.

Suzanne got up to freshen their drinks, and Harvey gave James an inquisitive look. "Are we still OK here?"

"Absolutely," replied James. "I think we might have a pretty good time tonight, if you are game for it."

"I'm game for about anything. You two seem to have the rulebook, so I will follow your lead and see what happens," replied Harvey.

Suzanne returned and sat down between them. They again toasted a successful week. Suzanne reached over to the front of James's pants and playfully squeezed him. "My goodness, you seem to be ready to play," she noted as James's erection grew exponentially. She then reached over to Harvey with the same results.

She skilfully pulled both belt buckles open almost simultaneously and carefully pulled down the zippers. She took James's erect organ into her mouth and playfully gave it a few strokes. She then turned to Harvey, exposing an equally magnificent erection, and proceeded to give it a few playful pulls.

At first, Harvey was very nervous and somewhat embarrassed about the situation. He was not quite certain how he was supposed to respond.

James interceded. "She really is the best. Enjoy, and all three of us will have a fabulous time. The bedroom would be far more comfortable at this point."

Suzanne slowly took off her sweater, fully revealing what Harvey had been lusting after all evening. He was even more impressed when she dropped her skirt. She was wearing no underwear, standing totally nude for both men to fully enjoy. By any criteria, Suzanne was gorgeous with coal black hair; large, firm, silicone-enhanced breasts; a flat belly; and just a fringe of well-trimmed black pubic hair. She had no piercings.

"Why don't you guys get rid of your clothes? And let's take a quick shower just to get rid of all the courtroom smell."

The shower was huge with two showerheads at each end, all marble and glass with gold fixtures. Suzanne adjusted both showers to a warm, pulsating flow, and she proceeded to generously lather herself and both men with body wash until they were slick and soapy. She was superbly adept at stroking and massaging every part and was equally enjoying being stroked soaped and explored.

"OK, boys. Let's get those two things out of the way before somebody gets injured." She proceeded to set the body soap aside and rinse off. "It's well past my bedtime." She laughed.

They towelled dry, and Suzanne pulled the bed covers off of the huge, oversized bed.

She lay down on the bed, partially spreading her legs, "Anybody want to play?"

Both men were beside her, fondling her breasts, kissing her face and neck, running their hands through her thick black bush, and feeling the wetness between her lips. She held both of their erect organs and slowly stroked.

She rolled over on top of Harvey, mashing both of her breasts firmly against his chest. She settled her pelvis directly over his throbbing organ, which without hesitation or need for direction promptly slipped into her vaginal orifice and buried itself to the hilt. She slowly undulated her pelvis, pushing the level of erotic sensation ever higher.

James, on his knees behind her, began massaging her anus, first slipping in one finger, then two, until she began to relax, which was difficult because she was still moving vigorously on top of Harvey. James pushed the head of his penis firmly and smoothly against her, and the reluctant muscles relaxed as his organ slipped in. Now both men were inside her, pushing in rhythm with her motions.

It was clear that both James and Harvey were very close to reaching climax when Suzanne, with two smooth movements, freed herself of both impaling organs and dropped back on the bed. "Let's take five to regroup. We have all night and don't want to waste it so soon."

She lay there, gently stroking both men, alternately licking and sucking on their swollen members with just enough control to prevent anything from going off. She then changed positions and moved to the head of the bed, straddling Harvey's face with her wet pelvis.

Harvey lay flat in bed. Suzanne straddled his face, gliding her vulvar lips up and down from nose to chin with his eager tongue ever present in the middle. James lay beside them and slightly down in the bed, holding and stroking Harvey's erect organ. He tentatively placed the head in his mouth, tasting the sweet, lubricating fluid copiously flowing from the opening. With no objection from Harvey, he pulled the organ deeper into his mouth and began slowly stroking it with his right hand. With his left hand, he massaged a generous amount of Astroglide around and into his anal opening. When he was satisfied that he had loosened the tight constricting ring sufficiently, he straddled Harvey, placing the head of his erect penis firmly against his still tight anal sphincter. With gentle downward pressure, he was able to achieve good relaxation, and the head of Harvey's penis pressed past his relaxing sphincter. The shaft followed full length into James's pelvis. He then started moving slowly up and down, keeping his pelvic muscles tight to enhance the sensation.

Harvey became so engaged in this new pleasure that he hardly noticed Suzanne moving to a position behind James. Almost in a choreographed movement, James lifted off of Harvey and scooted up his chest. Suzanne replaced him, taking Harvey's erect organ full depth into her pelvis, all of this seemingly without missing a stroke.

Suzanne continued her rhythmic dance. Harvey now realised that James was straddling his chest with his penis only inches away from his face. He reached out and began stroking the shaft of the slippery organ, curling his fingers around the head. He moved James farther up his chest until he took the head in his mouth, tasting the slick, sweet liquid while he continued to stroke the shaft.

Suzanne continued her undulating dance. The rhythm had significantly picked up until she advanced into a screaming orgasm, followed by short moments of relaxation and a cascading series of spasms of sheer ecstasy as she kept up the rhythmic motion.

The sensations that Harvey experienced, both from Suzanne's persistent motion and the fascinating novelty of tasting another man's organ, rapidly brought him to a climax. The beginning of an orgasm starts with a tingling and involuntary tightening of the muscles of the inner thighs. This is immediately followed by constriction of the pelvic muscles, which initiates the unstoppable, spasmodic contraction of the muscles around the prostate and seminal vesicles. The sequence takes only a few seconds from initiation to explosive orgasm. In a series of spasmodic ejaculations, Harvey released a week's worth of pent-up seminal fluids into the deepest recesses of Suzanne's vaginal vault.

James could not hold back any longer, and as Harvey began to relax from his intense pleasure, he reached orgasm, the head of his penis still in Harvey's mouth. Harvey eagerly savoured the viscous, alkaline fluid coursing in spasmodic ejections into his mouth, flowing over his tongue and down into his throat. Harvey's analytic physician's mind was trying to remember the pH and chemical composition of seminal fluids, but in any event, it was a very interesting flavour and sensation.

In the final piece of the choreography, Suzanne lifted off of Harvey and fell fully back onto the bed, legs wide apart. James immediately moved away from Harvey and into position between her legs. He buried his face into her wet pelvis, eagerly sucking the copious amounts of seminal fluid now draining from her vagina.

The three of them, now totally spent, lay in bed with Suzanne in the middle, still fondling the flaccid organs of each man.

Harvey finally broke the silence. "This may be something that you two do occasionally, but it has been a totally different experience for me. I had never even considered how much mixed pleasure having simultaneous sex with both a man and a woman can create. If it's OK with you two, I would like to try a rerun of this sometime in the future."

James replied, "The trial is on the docket for the first week in December and should last all week. I'm certain that you will be needed here in Portland throughout the trial, and you will probably be the last witness on the stand Friday afternoon."

Suzanne injected. "Speaking for myself, it has been a fabulous evening, absolutely superb sex. An encore in December must definitely be scheduled. Hopefully more than one performance. To make it even more interesting, I will see if Julie might like to participate and make it a foursome, which is really special."

Conclusion

In this chapter, we are investigating the extremely complex relationships that can occur when either partner of a marriage has the confidence in one's own sexuality to allow one's spouse to freely engage with another individual. James and Suzanne willingly invited another individual to share a three-way sexual experience. This activity should not be indiscriminately practiced, or else it degrades the value of the strong bonds of love that hold the couple together. Openly sharing everything with old or new friends, putting all common jealousies aside, can only enhance the experience for everyone. This clearly is not recommended for most couples because the average marriage would ultimately be torn apart by jealousies

Questions

1) Do you find the idea of a threesome acceptable?
2) What if the threesome was composed of two women and one man? Would you feel differently?
3) Can you accept anal sex as a component of a full sexual experience? Would you feel confident in refusing to participate in that variety (or any other kind) of sex if it was not acceptable to you?
4) As a man or a woman, would you find it difficult or awkward to watch your partner having sex with another individual?
5) What are your feelings about participating in group sex activity? Would you try this if the opportunity presented itself?
6) Do you think that extending the sexual experience beyond your partner would diminish your love for your partner? Could you ever feel the same again toward him or her?

CHAPTER 5

BIG JOHN AND MEGAN

Megan O'Reilly was about as Irish as one could get. With short dark hair and a spitfire temper, all 120 pounds of her would take on anybody if provoked. She was born in Dublin, Ireland, where she'd met her late husband, Patrick, while he was serving a tour of duty as a US MP at a nearby airbase. After six weeks of dating, they were married. She was eighteen, and Patrick was twenty-two. Ultimately, the tour of duty was over, and they returned to the United States.

Patrick was honourably discharged after eight years of service in air force security. He joined the Portland police force and rapidly worked his way up to detective. Two years ago, he was killed in a drug raid shoot out, leaving Megan with their three-year-old son. She has found it very difficult to make ends meet and take care of herself and her young son on only police and air force pensions. To complicate matters further, Patrick Junior was recently diagnosed with early signs of dyslexia.

Her first introduction to Big John was when she and Patrick would meet at Dooley's with some of the other police detectives for a late-evening get-together and a few drinks. After Patrick's death, she spiralled into the depths of depression, often stopping by Dooley's in the early afternoon when one of her friends would take care of Patrick Junior, PJ, for a few hours. She was drinking to ease the pain and depression, and after having watched her father literally drink himself to death, she worried—but not enough to stop drinking. Big John knew the symptoms all too well as he listened to her stories and her difficulty in finding a work schedule that would allow her to spend as much time as possible with PJ. She was currently working as a late-night stocker at the local Walmart three nights a week. Bad hours, poor pay, and it cost almost as much to have somebody watch PJ overnight as she made.

She and Patrick had made a number of very good friends, mostly within the police department during the six years that he had worked on the force. However, following Patrick's death, most of their friends quietly drifted away. The exception was Marie, who continued to stand by her and was a big help with PJ when she needed a few hours to herself. Marie would always say, "I already have three. One more does not matter."

With few friends and with no family support, she had to find a steady job that paid a reasonable wage and still allowed her to spend as much time with PJ as possible.

The day one of his cocktail waitresses quit, Big John offered her a position as a table attendant at Dooley's, and she eagerly accepted. He offered to let PJ stay in his living quarters on the second floor above the bar so he could do school work or sleep while Megan worked. Megan was eager to learn and quickly worked her way to bartender. After she had worked there for just over one year, John had developed so much confidence in her honesty and ability that for the first time in many years, he would take off a few evenings and allow her to run the place on her own. She did an excellent job. John slowly began to turn over many of the business aspects of running the bar to Megan, and she eagerly accepted the responsibility.

Aside from her work and caring for her son, Megan had no outside interests or activities. She was attractive enough to men, but she always mentioned her son as part of the relationship up front, which usually ended the relationship. Men love attractive women, but without baggage, and she had plenty of baggage in the form of a dyslexic, hyperactive five-year-old boy.

Big John had been married twice and had no children; there had been many intervening girlfriends, none for any extended period of time. His intense devotion to his business required his full attention for most of his waking hours, significantly hampering the social interaction that most women crave.

John was the only male child of Samuel Dooley, and by default he'd inherited Dooley's Bar and Grill. This had been the only life that John had ever known, and it was the only occupation that really made sense to him at all. His mother, whose entire life was devoted to caring for her family, died of breast cancer when John was only six years old. John, a devout Catholic, loved children and always hoped to someday have a large family. Now forty-five years into his life, it began to look less and less likely that this was going to happen.

Megan would apologise when she had to bring PJ to work, but John always assured her that PJ was not a burden and was really a ray of sunshine sent by God to brighten his life.

Megan lived within walking distance of Dooley's, and so getting back and forth to work was never a problem. She worked six nights a week, but she had most of the days off except when Big John needed her to help with bookkeeping, stocking, and frequent inventory of the bar.

Megan would usually come to the bar on Saturday morning. She would bring PJ with her and spend most of the day checking inventory, paying bills from the local vendors, filling out endless state and federal tax forms, and completing a host of other paperwork chores that were clearly beyond John's capability. The more she looked into the overall financial status of the bar, the more concerned she became with what appeared to be major discrepancies in cash flow. She clearly identified three upfront problems. Bar revenue was not matching bar inventory. Billing for food service was costing more than revenue. A drop in late-evening patronage, especially late in the week and through Saturday, was a new trend. It was not long until she had identified the cause of all three problems, and she confronted John with her conclusions.

"John, if you truly want me to help you in this business, you have to listen to what I tell you. You are great guy, a fantastic people person, and the best bartender one could ask for, but your business savvy really sucks. I know you cannot help but be aware that in spite of the fact that we seem to have good clientele and a good trade, the business is losing money.

"I like you a lot. I like working with you, but you absolutely are going to have to come to grips with reality. Your love life has been a disaster. You lost your home to your second wife, and you have made a succession of poor choices since that time. This is all past history, and I cannot fix your personal life. But there are three things that you could do right now that would significantly improve your business life and turn the business around, if you would let me institute them.

"First off, your early shift bartender, Billy, is absolutely ripping you off by milking the till. I have counted the drinks crossing the bar, and the cash flow reconciles only about 20 per cent of it ever hitting the cash register. Next, your food supplier is about as crooked as they come. He shorts you on the orders, the quality is substandard, and he often double-charges because he knows that you're not paying attention. I see the bills, and I know what we serve. The last problem, and one that you absolutely need to fix, is to get rid of obvious hookers who hang around here later in the evening and essentially drive off all the good customers. I know you don't like confrontation. Just give me the authority to handle this. I don't want any more pay. In fact, you cannot afford what you're paying me now. Just let me make some decisions for you."

John replied, "Megan, I hear what you're telling me, but I truly don't know what to say. I never even thought about these things. I just assumed everybody was dealing with me honestly. I have always been aware of the hookers. They are a fact of life in most bars, and everybody has to make a living somehow. I know your heart and mind are in the right place. Do what you think is best, and I will back you up."

Megan instituted the changes at John's, authority and the business cash flow immediately and dramatically improved. Megan rapidly earned a reputation around town of being a tough but very fair negotiator.

It was late Tuesday evening, one week before Thanksgiving. The weather outside was becoming miserable, with a brisk north wind and light snow falling. The last of the patrons had left by nine o'clock, and Megan suggested that they might as well close and end the day with a nightcap. Big John fully agreed, and he locked the front door, turned off the outside lights and the big neon sign in the window, that proclaimed Dooley's as the finest Irish pub in Portland.

They retreated to the upstairs living area to find PJ on the living room sofa sound asleep, covered with a bright red American Airlines blanket pilfered from some long-ago flight.

"He looks so peaceful that I hate to wake him up," said Megan.

"Then let's not wake him up for a while and celebrate whatever there is to celebrate," said Big John.

Megan retorted, "If nothing else, we are alive and healthy, and PJ is doing great. The business is dramatically improved since I made a few changes for us, and we both have jobs. I think we have a lot to celebrate."

"I'll drink to that," said Big John as he produced a bottle of fine Irish whiskey from a nearby cupboard, poured precisely three fingers into each of two glasses, and skilfully slid one across the table. The glass stopped dead centre in front of Megan.

Damn, he's good. I need to work on that technique, thought Megan.

They touched their glasses, and Big John saluted. "To those who are like us, but none are better than us."

John downed his in one swallow; Megan took a little bit longer, savouring the fiery liquor as it passed across her tongue and down her throat.

After the second three fingers, Big John was much mellower. He seldom drank very much, but tonight he wanted to relax. Megan had finished her first drink, and because she felt a little tipsy, she was slowly sipping on her second.

"Megan, you started working for me in April two years ago. In this brief period of time, you have learned everything there is to know about running the business. You are not only doing a superb job, but I think you really enjoy what you're doing."

"John, if it had not been for you rescuing me after Patrick's death, I honestly don't know what would've become of me. I was really down and out with no friends, no family except PJ, and no discernible future."

John continued. "What about your future and PJ's future? You can't work forever as a cocktail waitress and bartender."

"I really don't know. Right now things are pretty good, and none of us really knows what the future may hold. I may get married again someday, if I find the right person, but so far I have not run into any viable candidates. I would like to have some more kids, but Patrick and I were married almost nine years before PJ magically appeared. I may not be able to have any more children even if I do get married."

They were sitting at the table in John's combination living and dining area, watching PJ quietly sleeping on the couch, content, secure, and oblivious to all the trials of the world going on around him.

Big John broke the silence. "I love watching him sleep, and while you're working, I often come up here and check on him."

"I know you do," said Megan. "That, and so many other traits, makes you feel like family to me. In fact, you're the only family that I have outside of PJ."

"Megan, I've been married twice, and you know, I've had a bunch of really worthless girlfriends. But my feelings toward you are different. I think of you as family, but you really are not. I think of you as a friend, but I would hope more than a friend. And I must also consider you as someone who works for me, all of which is very conflicting and very confusing. Can you understand what I'm feeling and what I'm trying to tell you? Just getting to know you and PJ over the last two years has given me something to look forward to every day, which I have not had for a long time.

"I'm certainly not a role model. You remember the ill-fated episode with Andrea last year, who claimed to be part of a ballet dance troupe? Then I found out she was really a stripper and drink hustler working at Harry's over on Sixth Street?"

"Yeah, I remember her all too well. The last time she came in the bar, I wanted to serve her a poison drink, but I thought it would give the bar a bad reputation and so did not," Megan laughingly retorted.

"I would have been better off if you had. She was really bad news. But what I really want to tell you is that I either have bad taste or bad luck when it comes to selecting female companionship. You are the first person whom I have actually been able to associate with, in any fashion, on a steady basis for longer than one year without each of us wanting to kill the other one."

"John, I do not see you that way at all. You are extremely easy to work for and to work with. Perhaps it is the fact that both of us have strong Irish backgrounds, ethics, and principles. Honestly, I can't remember any cross words between us during this entire association. I love working at Dooley's. I feel totally at home with the business and the patron. I feel like I belong here."

"I have never made a pass at you, Megan, and you have never come on to me—which is highly unusual for the girls who normally work in a bar. I always thought of you more as an equal partner rather than an employee, and you treat your job at that level of respect and care. I have been thinking over the past few months of making you a partner in this business. You now know more about running Dooley's than I do. The patrons love you, and your personality and enthusiasm can really get things going on a slow Friday evening."

"John, is it the whiskey talking, or are you seriously making this offer to me? You caught me totally by surprise on that one. I am perfectly content to just work here. You pay me well, you treat me well, and more important, you accept PJ," replied Megan.

"Maybe some of it is the whiskey, which tends to unencumber people and allow them to say things and express their feelings without the constraints of political correctness or the standard rules of engagement. I think of this as a conversation between two people who obviously care for and respect each other."

"Don't get me wrong, John. This is more than I could have hoped for, and far more than I deserve. You have no obligation towards me, and I guess my obligation to you does not extend much beyond a thirty-day notice," explained Megan.

John fell silent for a few moments, picked up his empty whiskey glass, reached for the bottle, and then set the glass back down on the table, looking straight at Megan. "You must know that you mean more to me than just an employee. You have become a very important part of my relatively boring and routine existence. I look forward to every evening when you show up for work, PJ in tow. I hate it when you walk out the door at the end of the shift and go home, and I have to retreat into the back corner of my lonely existence. I realise you have no obligation to me, and the good Lord knows with my terrible track record, I cannot expect you to think of me in any fashion other than your boss."

"John, you are much too harsh on yourself. You may be big and tough on the outside, but I have seen your soft and tender side many times, and I do look at you as more than just a friend and my boss. I like you very much as a person. I like being around you. I like your funny side, and I like your tough side. And I love working with you. Perhaps all of this means more than the tenuous glue that holds most relationships together."

John reached across the table and took both of her hands in his huge paws. "Megan, is it possible that I love you? Could you ever look at me that way?"

"I don't know, John. I really have not thought that far ahead. Patrick has now been gone five years, and I never really gave much thought to including another man in my life with everything else that I have to be concerned about," she replied sadly.

They sat there in silence for many minutes, listening to a combination of snow and sleet being driven against the window as the wind outside picked up. PJ was still blissfully slumbering on the couch. The room was warm, the whiskey had been good, and the hour was late.

Megan slowly mulled over all of their conversation of the past hour. She got up and wrapped her arms around Big John, and buried her face in his chest, quietly sobbing. He held her tightly against him, gently stroking her short black hair.

"I'm sorry. I really did not mean to upset you this much," he apologised.

"I'm not upset. This is just an unembellished look at the reality of my life, and probably yours too. The two of us have met on a happenstance of fate, through no planning of our own, and as it so often happens, our destiny is being shaped by circumstances far beyond rational control.

"Love is a very difficult thing to define. In fact, it truly defies any sort of rational solid definition. It is a sense of belonging and a bond that develops between two people: same sex, opposite sex, mother and child, and the list continues, each with its own rules but always with the same outcome. You feel like you have known that person forever, and you are becoming part of that person, ultimately blending down to one individual. If you don't achieve that final bond, it will not be true, lasting love. Deep down, I know that I feel that way about you. Although neither of us ever openly expressed our feelings, they have been growing, and we have been subconsciously bonding for a long time."

Megan looked up into John's face. Standing twelve inches shorter than John, she stretched up to him. He slowly lowered his face down to hers until their lips touched. They slowly, tenderly explored what the next move for each of them might be.

After a few moments, she gently pulled away from him and held both of his hands. "This has been much more than I can get my mind around right now. What I would really like is for us just to lie down, and for you hold me in your arms until I go to sleep. I don't want to wake up PJ and have to walk home in the snowstorm. In fact, I don't want to walk home at all. I just want to stay here with you, if that's all right."

Big John took her hand, they made sure PJ was still covered, and they walked into the bedroom and kicked off their shoes. He pulled a blanket off of the chair and gently covered her as she lay down upon the bed.

"Please lie down beside me. I want to feel the security of being here with you as I go to sleep," she pleaded.

John curled up around her back, placed his enormous arm across her, and held her tightly to his chest as they drifted off to sleep.

Two weeks later, their wedding and the wedding reception were held in Dooley's. The bar was closed for the day, but from the number of invited guests who attended, one would think that half of Portland had turned out for the occasion.

Conclusion

This story illustrates an entirely different sequence of the development of love. John and Megan started as friends and coworkers, and they finally developed a bond and trust much stronger than most people develop in marriage. John had total trust in Megan and deeply loved her and her child, but he never expressed his feelings to her. Megan developed the same bond but could not close the circle.

For them, love slowly grew each day they were together, and they crossed the line at some point from just being friends to becoming soul mates, bonding, trusting, and respecting each other. Sexual love did not appear in the beginning, as is the usual case, but was the final commitment towards developing that permanent bond between two people when they are truly in love.

Questions

1) Do you think this kind of traditional love story still happens today? Is it boring or comforting for you to contemplate?

CHAPTER 6

NEVER TOO OLD TO LEARN

Nedra Wiggins just turned fifty-five years old and was really depressed. At this stage in her life, she had every material advantage one could ask for. She was a founding and successor partner of Moore, Wiggins, and Short, the oldest law firm in Portland, which had been started by her great-grandfather in 1905. She had a reputation for honesty and integrity and was known as one of the toughest female lawyers on the East Coast. Her services were still in high demand, and she was well compensated with her annual income in the seven figures. In spite of all this, she was never able to develop any type of lasting social relationship with men. Somehow, she had always chosen the wrong male companionship throughout her life, to the point where now she resigned herself to being what she laughingly but sadly referred to as a professional virgin.

Today had been especially depressing. A cold fall rain had drizzled off and on for most of the day. She currently had no active cases on the docket, and she was bored and lonely. On a whim, she had decided to stop by Dooley's and planned to have more than one drink before working her way home.

She knew that many of her associates and friends came here frequently to unwind and mix after work. She thought about a solid rule she lived by: never mix business with pleasure, which meant minimal social interaction with partners and employees—and clients were strictly off-limits. She knew that some of the other attorneys in the firm did not ascribe to this level of discretion, but she had her principles. They may be old-fashioned, but she was damn well going to stick by them.

Big John, the proprietor, owner, and chief bartender, greeted her with his rich Irish brogue. "And what will you have this evening, me lovely Miss Wiggins? You have not been by here for a while. Very glad to see you again. May I pull you a Guinness?" Big John was phenomenal in that he seemed never to forget customers and always knew what they usually ordered, no matter how infrequently they visited his bar.

She agreed to a glass of her favourite Guinness and continued to muse over the day and her life in general. *Being a professional virgin is a bitch,* she thought. Well, technically she wasn't a virgin. She had had pelvic exams throughout her medical lifetime, ending in a vaginal hysterectomy for endometrial hyperplasia, which was not really cancer but close enough to warrant the surgery, at the age of forty-five. *All the damn trouble those parts gave me over the years, and I never got any use out of them at all,* she lamented.

According to her gynaecologist, Rebecca Mansfield, her ovaries finally gave up at age fifty-two, resulting in endless bouts of hot flashes, some weight gain, and a general increase in her usual grouchiness. Because of this, her physician experimented with various combinations of hormones in an attempt to improve her physical and mental condition. She actually liked the current combination, which included a twice monthly medical cocktail injection of depo-testosterone, a male hormone; progesterone; a small amount of oestrogen; and a long-acting corticosteroid in the attempt to suppress her hot flashes and stabilise her mood swings.

Dr Mansfield had warned her that there might be some side effects, and if they became objectionable, she could rearrange the mix. Aside from feeling generally much better on the medications, Nedra had noted a little increase in hair growth, but the most astonishing thing was an increase in size and sensitivity of her completely unused and still remaining female part, her clitoris. She had read about it but was never really sure for what purpose God had designed this organ.

As she sat on the bar stool reminiscing and lamenting, a fast Irish folk dance played on the bar's background music system. She unconsciously kept time with the music, tapping her foot, which soon extended to bouncing her whole leg up and down to the beat. This soon evolved into a rhythmic, alternating motion of both legs while squeezing her thighs together, all of this undercover of the overhanging bar lip. This was beginning to develop a very warm, pleasant feeling in her pelvic area, which she involuntarily augmented by contracting her pelvic muscles in time with the music. As the tempo of the dance increased, she followed with more intense squeezing of her thighs and the muscles of the pelvic floor. The more she squeezed, the more pleasant the sensation she experienced. She could discern a warmth in her vulvar area that she did not recall ever feeling.

What in the hell is Dr Mansfield giving me? All of this is very unusual, but it feels amazingly good. I hope no one else in here is noticing me.

The tempo of the dance went on unabated, and the warmth and pleasure in her pelvis increased. She closed her eyes, and suddenly a totally unexpected wave of intense pleasure erupted from her pelvis, spread down her legs, and went up her spine. Her breathing became rapid and shallow, her heartbeat increased, and she was sure she was going to faint.

Big John noticed that she seemed to be having some trouble breathing, and he came to her and grasped both of her hands. "Miss Wiggins, Miss Wiggins, are you all right?"

She was startled back to reality and quickly replied, "I just felt dizzy for a moment. Perhaps I'm not used to drinking, but I'm still on my first one. I feel fine now; it passed just as fast as it came over me. My doctor changed my medication last month, and that might be related to the problem. I'm OK now—honestly, I feel fine. Thank you, John."

Son of a bitch, that was really weird, she thought. *I will sure ask Dr Mansfield about this one.* She then realised that her panties felt wet. *Damn! I hope I didn't lose bladder control during that seizure and pee my pants.*

She slipped off of the barstool and made a quick trip to the ladies' room to check out the situation. She was even more confused to find that she had not peed her pants but was secreting a clear viscous fluid which seemed to be coming from her vagina. *All very peculiar,* she thought. *This must be related to that new medication.*

She returned to the bar and found that John had brought her a fresh Guinness "Are you OK now?" he inquired.

"I'm OK now, no problem. In fact, I feel great," she replied.

She continued to mull over the events of the past few minutes, but still could not draw a logical conclusion as to what might had caused her to have such a strange, almost seizure-like sensation. *Maybe I need to go see Dr Furrer to see if I need an MRI or something.*

Dr Kevin Furrer was an internal medicine physician a few years older than Nedra, and he had been her family doctor for many years. She had last seen him just over a year ago for a general check-up, and she was told that she was fine at that time but needed to continue seeing Dr Mansfield about her hot flashes.

She recalled that Kevin's wife, Helen, had left him about two years ago, after three grown children and over thirty years of marriage. The divorce was handled by her firm and was relatively uncontested. Helen Furrer claimed to have fallen in love with a much older man, a retired local banker without a wife (and with plenty of money) who wanted to travel the world and asked her to be his companion.

Nedra had consulted on the case but declined to get involved because of a long-standing friendship with Helen and her professional relationship with Kevin.

She glanced up in the mirror and was startled to see Dr Kevin Furrer slowly working his way through the crowd, approaching her. She then realised that he had been sitting at the other end of the bar, and only a few moments earlier, he had been in deep conversation with Big John.

"Damn! John ratted me out. The last thing I need is a medical consultation at a bar."

He walked up to her and placed a warm hand on her shoulder. "Are you doing OK? John said you were having some problems breathing a few minutes ago."

"I'm OK now. I did have some sort of a strange, seizure-like experience a while ago. I don't think I lost consciousness, but I did feel like I was going to faint. But it has totally passed, and I feel fine. I was actually considering giving you a call next week to see if you thought perhaps an MRI might be in order." She then changed the subject. "What brings you in here? I didn't know you frequented places like this."

"Actually, I'm a regular in here now. I get in perhaps two to three nights a week. Big John and I always have a lot to talk about. But as you now mentioned it, I don't recall ever seeing you in here before."

"It's been a long time since I last stopped by here," Nedra replied. "It has been a long tough week and a tough day. My associates tell me this is a good place for post-work therapy."

She had been seeing Kevin professionally for many years, as a patient, but she'd never thought of him socially. He'd been married during the majority of this time, and any further contact outside of the office setting had never occurred to her.

While he talked to her, she carefully observed him for the first time as a person, not as her family physician. Kevin was not particularly handsome, but in a distinguished way he was very attractive to Nedra. Salt-and-pepper hair; a small gray, bushy, but well-trimmed moustache; silver wire-rim glasses, and perhaps a few extra pounds. *What the hell am I thinking? I'm an old, fat, frumpy, and often unpleasant lawyer.*

Kevin sat down on the stool beside her. "Mind if I join you for a drink? We can discuss your symptoms a little more, if you like."

"No, great, uh, yes, of course," she stammered, startled back to reality. "I mean, sure, have a seat. In fact, I'm glad to see you. As I mentioned earlier, I was going to call your office for an appointment next week."

"I normally don't make house calls at Dooley's, but for you I will make an exception, and since there is no Medicare place of service modifier to use for a bar, this visit will be free of charge," he joked.

"Stop that! I'm serious." She quietly explained the rapid breathing, increased heart rate, and a just as rapid subsidence of all symptoms. She made no mention of her strange pelvic sensations.

"Describe in detail exactly what happened," Kevin asked.

"Dammit, Kevin. Doctors always ask patients to describe exactly what happened. If I knew what happened, I would know what happened!"

"OK, what were you doing just before the episode occurred?" Kevin inquired.

"I was having a drink, halfway through my first Guinness, which is not excessive; I generally have one or two glasses of wine at home in the evening."

"What else happened?" Kevin persisted.

"I don't feel comfortable discussing this at the bar. Can we go sit at a booth?" suggested Nedra.

"Great idea," said Kevin. "And it is certainly more HIPAA compliant."

They moved to a booth in the back corner. Only one other couple was close by in an adjacent booth, and they were obviously more interested in each other than their surroundings.

"OK, I was tapping my foot in tune with an Irish folk dance that John was playing on the sound system."

"Has Dr Mansfield changed your medicines over the past few months?"

"Yes, she has me on depo-testosterone, progesterone, some oestrogen, and a long-acting corticosteroid. I get a shot every two weeks; usually her nurse gives it to me."

"Has this caused any side effects that you can recall?"

This is really getting way too deep for bar talk, she thought. "I may have had little increase in some hair growth, and I think I gained some weight."

"Anything else?"

Damn, he is persistent! she thought. They were interrupted by Megan, who usually tended bar, but John must've sent her over to the table with two more drafts.

"John says these two are on the house," said Megan with her thick Irish brogue. She was even more difficult to understand than big John.

After the interruption, Nedra changed the subject, and they drifted off into politics, both local and national, finding that they thought the same.

Kevin enjoyed being with Nedra and found her to be delightfully conversational and obviously well informed on most subjects. The exception was her recent episode, for which he was slowly formulating a diagnosis, but he needed a few more answers. *She does not appear to be anywhere near as tough as people see her on the courtroom floor,* he thought.

He continued to observe her closely while she talked. A little overweight, but so was he. Short and stylish gray hair, a pretty face, and a full figure. Strange that he had never thought of her in any way other than as a patient. Another fast Irish folk dance played, and he noticed her keeping time by tapping a leg with the tempo of the music.

"Were you doing that a while ago before you had your episode?"

"Well, yes, sort of."

"What is sort of?"

"Kevin, this is not a courtroom."

"No, and it really is not an examination room, but I am betting that I can come up with a diagnosis after a few more questions, if you will answer me directly and honestly."

"What do you mean by directly and honestly? I brought this whole thing up in the beginning, so I am damn well going to tell you a straight story."

"OK. Were you squeezing your legs together in time with the music?"

"Yes, I guess I was. I really never thought that had any connection to what happened."

"And did you increase the squeezing as the tempo of the dance increased?"

"I think I probably did."

"And that was about the time you had the shortness of breath, rapid heartbeat, and faintness feeling?"

"I never fainted—I just felt very lightheaded. I was having a hard time breathing, and my heart was racing."

"OK, one last but very important question. Did you feel anything unusual in your pelvic or female area?"

"Thinking about it now, that sensation was what started all the rest of my symptoms. Do you know what's causing it?"

"Nedra, to the best of my medical interpretation, I think you just experienced your first orgasm."

"What?" she almost shouted. "What are you insinuating?"

The people at the next table looked up at her sudden outburst but then resumed their conversation.

"I'm sorry, but isn't an orgasm something that men have during sex?" she replied much more quietly.

Kevin explained, "I'm insinuating nothing. That was a very natural experience that is frequently reported in younger women who perform some type of repetitive leg motion while seated. This was first reported in the nineteenth century in clothing factories, where women operated treadle sewing machines by foot. The repetitive leg motion constantly stimulated their genitals. The managers would notice what they termed "runaway sewing machine operators", which happened when the women were reaching an orgasmic peak. It is a known syndrome. Therefore in my expert medical opinion, the repetitive leg motion caused you to reach an orgasm, and the combination of medication that Dr Mansfield has you on at the present time is contributing to a dramatic increase in your libido."

"I never had a libido."

"Well, it sounds like you have one now. You probably needed one, but the question is what you're going to do with it."

"I have no idea, but this conversation has become very uncomfortable to me," said Nedra.

"I'm sorry," said Kevin. "This certainly is enough clinical evaluation tonight. I fear I have overstepped my bounds as your friend, but perhaps I'm still within the boundary as your physician."

"I too apologise," said Nedra. "You've given me a lot to think about tonight. Would you consider another office visit tomorrow night?"

"Same time, same place?" replied a surprised Kevin.

"Same booth, 6 p.m. This time I'm going to have some questions for you after I research this subject some more."

"Just don't believe everything you read on the Internet," advised Kevin. He paid the bar tab, and they went their separate ways home, both with a lot to think about.

The following evening, when Nedra came in to Dooley's, Kevin was already at the booth they had occupied the previous night. Nedra had not felt this young and free in many years—or perhaps ever. She was wearing make-up, and she had gone to the beauty salon and had her hair cut and styled today. Her nails were polished, and she wore a skirt and low-cut blouse.

Kevin spotted her immediately when she came through the door and watched her as she made her way across the room, taking a very long second look at her. *I never saw her before as anyone other than a casual acquaintance, and of course as a patient. She is a very attractive lady to me.* This was the first time since his wife had left him that he had even considered having a date. *Well, I guess this is a date. Every eligible female acquaintance of my age is looking for the security of marriage and somebody to accompany them to social functions. I think this is different. What am I fantasising about? This will obviously go nowhere.*

Kevin immediately stood up and helped her to her seat, this time sitting on the same side of the booth with her rather than across the table. Megan had observed Nedra walk in the door, had already drawn two pints of Guinness, and was on her way to the table with them.

Kevin opened the conversation. "It is great to see you again this evening, Nedra. You really look fantastic. You must be feeling much better today."

"I never really felt bad yesterday. In fact, I hate to admit it, but after your explanation that it was an act of nature and not a heart attack or stroke, I quit worrying about it altogether and wrote it off as a pleasurable event worth repeating."

After a few minutes of preliminary small talk, during which neither was very interested in the answers, Nedra revisited the subject.

"I did some research on orgasms, and I'm still confused. I always thought it was a man thing when he ejaculated, and that it had something to do with pregnancy and having children," she explained.

"Well, some yes, and a lot of no. Actually, women have more frequent and more intense orgasms than men. Most men have one, and then they are done; they rarely have more than two during any one session of intimacy. You are correct in that the orgasm in a man is almost always accompanied by ejaculation. Women do not have that mechanism, but they do experience a marked increase in vaginal fluid formation during that time. Nature has designed it this way, to improve the ability of sperm to survive, resulting in pregnancy.

"A woman commonly will have more than one orgasm if her companion is considerate, waits for her, and encourages her. Some women can have as many as twenty in one session of intercourse," Kevin patiently explained with great scientific precision.

"Holy shit," Nedra blurted out. "That would kill me. Actually, what I mean is that it was such an intense feeling, I can't imagine doing it multiple times."

"In all honesty, Nedra, do you really think, or can you ever recall, that you never had this experience before?" Kevin asked with great sincerity.

"Never. I was raised in a very strict family situation, and sex was never mentioned. As you know, my father was a very intense person absolutely dedicated to his profession, to the detriment of a solid family life. I recall asking my mother about sex when some of the girls at school were talking about it. She became almost violent and said that sex was nasty and the only purpose God had for it was to have children. She had given birth to one, and that was enough. Needless to say, I studiously avoided the subject forever.

"I guess sex is something that I put in the back of my head and suppressed. With all of the warped rules that have been imposed upon me since I was a young child, it became a way of life. I would turn away when any of my friends in college or law school talked about their sexual escapades—a sure route to becoming a professional virgin."

Kevin laughed out loud at that last remark. "I had never heard that term before, but I can certainly see how your childhood had a significant influence on you as you grew up into an adult."

"Kevin, you have examined me as a patient. Only a few years ago, as you may recall, I was having severe abdominal pain, and after you examined me, you sent me to see Dr Mansfield, who did the hysterectomy. Did you see anything else abnormal with me at that time?"

"I clearly recall your clinical situation from that time, but honestly, as a doctor I see so many patients that I remember only the pathology and quickly erase the rest of the examination."

Nedra explained, "After our discussion last evening, and after I had read somewhat on the subject, I thought that maybe I could re-create the situation at home to observe it in more detail. It didn't work. Do you have any suggestions?"

Where on earth is this going? thought Kevin as he dizzily tried to tie all of this to his sudden new feelings and interest towards her. *It is almost as though she is coming on to me.* "You have caught me completely off guard. I don't really know what to say," he stammered.

"Kevin, I don't really know how to say this, so in my usual blunt fashion, I will just come out with it. I find you very attractive, in fact more so than any man I think I've ever known. I am embarrassed to admit this, and I know this is very uncharacteristic of me."

"Nedra, this is certainly the first time that I have ever looked at you other than as a patient, except for the time that you helped me with some legal issue dealing with a medical supply firm. So I have no idea which direction any of this is going."

"You know my personality and that I am blunt and to the point. Would you even consider helping an old maid lawyer who is a quasi-virgin discover the joys she has been missing for all of these years?" Nedra asked.

This had taken another really fast and weird turn, thought Kevin. "Nedra, I am far from the expert in these matters. In fact, I am seriously lacking in any type of broad sexual experiences. I think my recent ex-wife had the same type of mother, or at least went to the same church your mother did. Sex was a duty to be performed, not enjoyed. We had three children, which were carefully timed, and I never ventured outside of our marriage."

"Actually, so much the better," said Nedra. "With a clean slate, we can make up the rules, right?"

"Madam, are you propositioning me?"

"Sir, I most certainly am. Neither one of us is getting any younger, and I am positive that I have missed a great deal in life."

"Your place or mine?" Kevin asked with a grin.

"Mine, so that if it does not go down well, I'm home. And if it goes very well, I'm still home," she said with authority. "I am illegally parked out in front in a white 550 SL, but the police gave up a long time ago writing me tickets. Follow me. I live in Worthington Estates, which is about ten miles north of town on state Highway 88, just off US 1.

"Yes I know that area. I've been there at social functions in the past with Helen."

"Stay with me, because security is very tight, and I will have to get you through the front gate," explained Nedra.

A short drive later, they cleared the guard post and passed through the huge iron gate and into a luxurious private enclave of elegant homes on expansive lots built along the cliff face overlooking the ocean. Kevin closely followed Nedra up her driveway and through yet another coded gate to her home.

The house was Tudor style, beautifully designed and set on a superbly manicured lawn. They parked in the circular driveway in front, and Nedra used a card key to open the door. The card key again plus a code on a concealed keypad deactivated the alarm system.

No sooner had they stepped into the entryway than the backup security system approached with a low, menacing snarl from a side room. Kevin froze in his tracks as a sixty-pound German shepherd confronted him, teeth barred with a rumbling growl emanating from his throat.

"Monarch, this is Dr Furrer. He is a friend," was all she needed to say. Monarch sniffed at Kevin's outstretched hand, gave a quick lick, and retreated back to his watch station just off the front hall.

"You really have a lot of security," remarked Kevin.

"That's not all," Nedra said, as she produced a Ruger 9 mm Luger pistol from her purse. "There are also equally as effective weapons concealed in almost every room in his home, and I know how to use all of them very well. In my days, I have made many very powerful friends—and unfortunately an equal number of very powerful enemies. I can't be too careful."

Reassured, Kevin took in the paintings and fixtures in the huge entryway. Nedra led the way into a magnificently appointed living area with wide expanse of glass looking directly out onto the Atlantic.

"You must be starved," she said. "We have spent the whole evening and never thought about getting anything to eat. Ingrid, my housekeeper, always fixes something for my dinner that can be warmed up when I get home. She always cooks as though I'm bringing home a group of friends, so I am sure that we will have plenty to eat. Make yourself at home, there should be a bottle of Silver Oak Cabernet on the bar. If you will pour us two glasses, I will put our dinner in the microwave."

She returned a few moments later, took Kevin's hand, and led him over to the picture window. "This is one of my favourite places. The sunrise is magnificent coming up over the Atlantic. In the state of Maine we get to witness the sunrise before anyone else in the United States." She motioned to a small table off to the side. "Have a seat, and I will bring our dinner out promptly."

She returned with a fully appointed tray, which she placed in front of Kevin. She soon returned with a similar tray for herself. The dinner was laid out on fine china with heavy silverware, which complemented the two crystal goblets that Kevin had discovered on the bar and appropriately filled with the cabernet.

"What are we having?" asked Kevin.

"I'm never really sure what Ingrid will fix from one day to the next. This appears to be beef tips in a burgundy sauce over basmati rice with baby limas to the side. The salad is sliced artichoke and hearts of palm over romaine with a balsamic dressing," she announced with the efficiency of a head waiter proclaiming the special of the evening.

"Very good selection. I think I will have that," replied Kevin with a chuckle as he raised his glass to hers in a toast.

"May this be the beginning of a long and fruitful relationship."

They toasted and savoured the deep, rich flavour of the wine, now looking at each other with a perspective of a reacquaintance born only twenty-four hours ago.

Dinner was quickly disposed of, with most of the conversation initiated by Kevin, who asked questions about her home.

"As you probably know, my great grandfather started his law practice in Portland in a small storefront office on Second Street just off the wharf in 1905. My grandfather founded our present law firm in 1927 by merging with two other local firms to form Moore, Wiggins, and Short. My father built this house in 1947, and as his only child, I grew up here and eventually inherited the property. The majority of the furnishings are original; I have changed very little about the house. I'm sure that the paintings and collectables are worth a fortune, but I have never bothered to have anything appraised. With no heirs, I have set up an elaborate trust to dispose of my estate in an orderly fashion, and of course as you are aware, I heavily contribute to the local arts."

As she cleared the table, she indicated that Kevin should refill their glasses, and they would tour the rest of the house.

The home was magnificent and beautifully laid out with original oil paintings, bronzes, and other collectables occupying wall space, tables, shelves, and nooks in almost every room. A central staircase rose from the foyer, dividing midway up and leading to a gallery surrounding the two-storey atrium. The last room she led him into was the master bedroom, with floor-to-ceiling glass and a view out over the Atlantic.

Kevin took off his jacket and undid his tie, draping both of them carefully across the back of a small loveseat in front of the window.

She held both of his hands, gazed into his face, and said, "I am really nervous. I have never even considered doing anything like this before, and I haven't a clue what the next step should be."

"I'm likewise woefully inadequate and unprepared, but perhaps a preliminary kiss would be a good beginning," offered Kevin.

He slowly and gently folded her into his arms, turned her face up towards him, and lightly pressed his lips against hers. They held this way for a few seconds, and he tentatively glided his tongue across her closed lips, testing for response.

He could feel her heartbeat steadily increasing as she willingly opened her lips, uncertain what would next take place. Kevin tenderly and hesitantly explored the front of her mouth with his tongue, touching and gliding along the tip of her tongue as the two secondary organs of sexuality greeted each other and began a mating ritual as old as time itself. Instinct took over where experience was lacking.

Kevin tightened his grip around her, his hands caressing through her short gray hair, and she held his head firmly as their preliminary exploration continued uninterrupted for many minutes.

When they finally drew apart, Nedra breathlessly confessed that she had never experienced a kiss of that intensity and intimacy in her entire lifetime. "If that is all there is to it, I will take it and never ask for anything more."

"Actually, "Kevin said, "that can be repeated multiple times, but there is much more, each step of which elevates the pleasure of the experience."

"Teach me. You are never too old to learn," confessed Nedra.

"First, let's set the mood. I think I have found the lighting controls," he said as he decreased the light intensity in the room. He found the stereo control unit, pressed CD, and was rewarded with new age Windham Hill playing softly from concealed speakers. "I like your taste in music I would've never suspected. I would've thought you to be more into the classics."

"I love the classics, the system has over one thousand CDs in it. One can select by genre, but I really like some of the new age music."

Kevin placed his hands on her shoulders, and they repeated their exercise in oral exploration, this time with greater intensity and passion. Nedra reciprocated by pressing her tongue far into Kevin's willing mouth.

When they broke apart the second time, Kevin allowed his hands to drift casually down across her ample bosom. He could detect a shiver of delight as his hands passed across her breasts. She made no move to resist, and caressing passed on to what Kevin referred to as the medical term of palpation.

"I recall this from a previous office visit, Doctor Furrer," said Nedra. "But this feels infinitely better."

"I reserve this technique only for special cases. In fact, this is about as special as a case can get," replied Kevin.

He gently kneaded her breasts and slowly unbuttoned the front of her blouse, eventually finding his way obstructed by a very sturdy bra.

She followed his lead, slowly unbuttoning his shirt one button at a time.

Kevin slipped her blouse down over her shoulders, and it fell to the floor. He then released the catch on her bra, and it slipped forward. She lowered her arms and leaned forward, and it fell to the floor too, revealing firm, perfectly symmetrical breasts.

He caressed the soft, smooth, unblemished white skin, gently skimming across her erect nipples. He eventually dipped down and carefully kissed one and then the other.

Nedra was beside herself at this point and was now experiencing intense reactions from another secondary sexual organ. She eagerly pressed his face against her breasts as he took one nipple at a time into his mouth, carefully caressed it with his tongue, and then sucked on it.

The intensity of the arousal that she felt was rising with each motion that he made. She began to feel the same constricting powerful sensation arising in her pelvis, spreading down her legs and up her spine, terminating in her nipples, which she was sure were on fire. Her orgasm exploded with far more intensity than she had experienced the previous day. She let it all go, pressing Kevin against her chest and screaming out in ecstasy as wave after wave of intense feelings coursed through her body.

Finally Kevin relented and released her as she stood there shaking from the intensity of the experience.

"My god, Kevin. That was absolutely unbelievable. I'm glad I didn't do that at Dooley's."

"Me too. It would've probably gotten us thrown out. That's the top half. The bottom half becomes even more interesting and intense." Kevin replied with a smile.

"Is that even possible?" asked an incredulous Nedra.

"Well, we've come this far. Let's find out. So far neither one of us has died from the experience." Kevin led her over to the bed, and the two of them pulled down the covers. "OK, this is the nasty part your mother talked about. Not only is it not nasty, but I promise you that you will find that the next chapter of your erotic educational course will be superbly satisfying."

First he undid the clasp and lowered the zipper on her skirt, allowing it to fall to the floor and leaving her clad only in her white silk panties.

He got down on his knees in front of her and slowly moved his face back and forth across her still protected belly. He could feel the heat and scent arising from her pelvic area. He carefully put a finger under each side of the waistband of her panties and slowly pulled them down, revealing a luxurious auburn bush now laced with silver.

Nedra stood there breathing heavily, her eyes closed and her hands on both sides of his head, making no move to resist his advances as he slowly moved his face back and forth across her lower abdomen.

He stood up and released his belt, unzipped his pants, and allowed them to fall to the floor. This was followed by his shorts, revealing the best erection he could remember in many years. He stood there not moving for a moment to allow Nedra to adjust to the rapidly escalating events of the evening.

So far, she had averted her gaze from what was taking place in front of her, but eventually she could not stand it any longer and looked down upon the first male erection she had ever observed. The sight was terrifying and at the same time intensely fascinating.

"This is a totally new experience. May I touch it?"

"I would hope that you would. This is all part of Erotica 101, a beautiful experience when done properly."

She gingerly touched the erect organ with two fingers and then with her whole hand, squeezing and exploring the shape and size of this completely foreign anatomic appendage. She noted the clear, slick fluid emanating from the opening and remarked, "Is that the same stuff that was running out of my vagina yesterday?"

Kevin laughed at her openness." Yes, basically. It's for the same purpose of lubrication and sperm protection."

"Can I look at this closer?" She got down on her knees in front of him. She held his erect organ in her hand and smoothed the slick fluid over the head, amazed that more kept coming out. "I would like to taste it and put it in my mouth. Is that acceptable?"

"Oh, more than acceptable," agreed Kevin.

She wrapped her lips around the head of his penis and gently caressed it with her tongue. *I could really get to like this in a hurry,* she thought.

Kevin gently lifted her up and indicated that they could lie down on the bed much more comfortably. They proceeded to return to another long, deep, and passionate kiss, which she responded to by pressing her body firmly against his.

Their lips parted, and Kevin proceeded to move back down to her breasts, which he continued to caress, squeeze, and kiss, quickly bringing her to another screaming orgasm.

"Good god, Kevin," she sighed breathlessly. "If there is more to this lesson, I don't know that I can stand it."

"There really is some more, and I would bet that you will be able to stand it. I promise that based on the experience of the past few minutes, you're going to really enjoy it."

He then moved his kissing and caressing farther down her abdomen until he again reached the heavy thatch of auburn hair at her pubis. This time, however, he did not stop. He continued to move back and forth and progressively downward until his tongue reached her enlarged clitoris. He began to slowly stroke back and forth across the erect organ, and he immediately brought her to another screaming climax.

"Shit, shit, holy shit!" she screamed "An entire lifetime of deprivation has just been dramatically overturned. You've got to stop for a few minutes so I can recover."

Kevin moved back up alongside of her and continued to slowly caress her soft belly, breasts, and neck. His hard, hot, erect organ firmly pressed against the side of her thigh. He slowly and carefully lifted up over on top of her. Her legs were already wide apart, and he slowly allowed his penis to slip smoothly into her tight but willing vagina. The results were almost instantaneous, rewarded with another screaming and thrashing orgasm. He slowly began to push in and out, pausing every few moments in sympathy with her heightened sensitivity, but always persistently pressing firmly against her. She experienced repeated orgasms about every fifteen seconds, and by his observations she was probably approaching her maximum limit, whatever that would be.

Kevin could hold back no longer and erupted into his own violent climax, now blended with her most recent one, until his painfully swollen prostate and seminal vesicles had relieved themselves of their pent-up accumulation of seminal fluid.

After a few minutes, he withdrew from her, and they lay back side-by-side, wrapped in each other's arms, totally spent by the overwhelming experience.

Kevin quipped, "I must remember to send Dr Mansfield an office note regarding the success of her menopausal correction cocktail."

"No way in hell is anybody going to know about this" Nedra emphatically stated.

"OK," said Kevin. "How about this? 'After a careful clinical evaluation and examination, it is my opinion that the patient's postmenopausal symptomatology has dramatically improved under her current medical regimen. I would recommend continuing the drugs and dosage as prescribed. The patient is to return as needed. Kevin Furrer, MD.'"

"That should work, as long as I can continue participating in your clinical experiment."

"That's a promise."

Conclusion

The purpose of this chapter is to illustrate that love truly has no age limits. Youths generally thinks that they invented love, or lovemaking, because it's one of the first things that they discover in late adolescence or early adulthood. People sometimes completely miss the opportunity to love or be loved because of extenuating circumstances. Situations can arise because we create them, or through no fault of our own, and ultimately cause us to erect a protective wall around our psyche, preventing others from entering our space.

Nedra is such a person. Through no real fault of her own, but just a series of bad choices early in life, she never found the match for which she was looking. Ultimately she resigned herself to a category that she described as a "professional virgin", a term that she utilised to degrade herself. Because of a long,-term, comfortable relationship with Dr Furrer, she allowed this wall to crumble and the two of them ultimately were able to discover a fulfilling and lasting relationship. Where both of them felt that the spectre of advancing age would prohibit such a relationship, they discovered that it truly can work if two people can nurture the attractive force between them.

Questions

1) Do you like Nedra?
2) Do you think it's possible for a woman to reach Nedra's age without ever experiencing an orgasm, even by accident?
3) What about a doctor dating a patient? Where should a line be drawn between professional and personal interaction? Is Kevin's and Nedra's relationship appropriate?
4) What would happen in a small community where nearly every resident is a patient of the only doctor?

CHAPTER 7

LARRY AND RONNIE

By all definitions, Larry Hansen was a true computer nerd. His ability with numbers had always been his strong suite and his nemesis. He had no other skills, social or otherwise. He was, however, clearly a league above all the other programmers at MBI, a software development firm in Portland. His expertise covered the required spectrum of programming languages such as Sybase, SQL, Dicom, and a host of other programs and routines.

This cold November morning, Larry was in his windowless cubicle facing three forty-inch monitors arranged in a semicircle across his desk. He had just entered the final command into the powerful Dell mainframe computer and was watching a blur of numbers race across all three screens. The program compiled the final version of an algorithm which, if it worked, would allow MBI to analyze the full DNA patterns of over ten thousand postpartum women. The data was being extracted from blood samples of the mothers and their newborn infants. The purpose of the program was to extract the DNA code sequence from each case, looking for a single elusive aberration that was causing a fatal birth defect in a small number of newborn infants. The entire project was being sponsored by a large federal grant and was supervised by the local medical school.

Unknown to anyone else at MBI, the system was also working in a multilevel, password-protected, compartmentalised section of the enormous processor on a special pet project of Larry's. He was getting very close to breaking the code of the program that developed the random numbers for the state lottery. Larry knew every winning combination that had been drawn since the inception of the state lottery program, not only Maine's but seven other states that, based upon the sequence of numbers, appeared to be utilising the same program.

He now had achieved the accuracy of predicting the winning combination down to the last set of numbers, meaning that he could now predict four of the five numbers almost every time. By his best estimate, he should be able to make the final prediction of the fifth number within a certainty of one out of ten after thirteen more weeks of drawings. The bonus multiplier number still remained elusive.

So far, all of this had been nothing more than a numbers game to him. He wanted to see if he could reproduce the program that generated the random numbers. Although he made a very good salary and had minimal expenses, he still could not resist the temptation to routinely purchase ten lottery tickets per week, always at different convenience stores. Invariably, at least one of these would win well over one thousand dollars.

As he watched the numbers cascade across the three screens, his thoughts drifted to the big payday, which might be only thirteen weeks away. Then what? He did not know what he would spend the money on. He presently had a nice apartment, no car, no pets, and no real significant other.

No significant other. His thoughts moved on to Ronnie, who had disappeared from his life 13 months, 3 days, 10 hours, and 15 minutes ago, or about 34,322,400 seconds. *Why the hell do I always do things like that worthless but interesting calculation? Best answer is because I can.* The bottom line was that Ronnie was probably gone for good. They had been in Dooley's, and Ronnie had struck up an intimate conversation with a man sitting at the bar. They had left together, and Ronnie had never returned. Larry had reported Ronnie's disappearance to the police the next day, but it was dismissed as a lover's quarrel and not worth their time to investigate unless he had more proof of foul play. As he heard one police sergeant say when he thought he was out of earshot, "Just another typical queer deal gone bad. Not worth wasting our time investigating it."

Larry never really thought of himself as a homosexual. He liked women to talk to and look at, but he was extremely insecure with them otherwise. He felt much more comfortable in the company of men, and especially Ronnie, who made him feel special. Ronnie had drifted outside of their comfortable social circle of two guys, he and Larry, and 2 girls Cheryl and Sherrill, who are bisexual, but declared openly lesbian, and Renée, who is half-and-half and ambivalent about it. Renée was a totally beautiful female above the belt and was still very male below the belt. This small group had always made a point of watching out for each other, but that particular evening, against all warning signs, Ronnie had left with an unknown person.

Larry continued to think of Ronnie as truly a beautiful person, with long, blond, well-styled hair; a beautiful face; and a body to die for. Ronnie would now be 29 years, 3 months, and 5 days old. Larry realised he could not calculate the rest because he did not know the exact birth time. *Make a note to ask Ronnie's mother if she knows what time he was born.*

Larry was of average build but nothing exceptional, with some well-trimmed facial hair and no tattoos or piercings. Admittedly, he did not push his body like Ronnie, who was a bodybuilder and utilised steroids for muscle development. In spite of a phenomenal body, he always played the girl, with Larry taking the role of the dominant partner. Much of this was due to testicular atrophy caused by high doses of anabolic muscle-building steroids, resulting in male hormone suppression. *He might as well have been a girl. God, how I miss that body,* Larry thought.

The screens flashed, and the system indicated that it had successfully compiled the latest iteration of the program. Now for the big test. He pulled up the massive DNA database and inserted the proper commands to allow full access. The screens again flashed, and endless rows of code scuttled across the three monitors. "Access approved. Compilation in progress." Now another long, agonising wait to see if it would successfully begin the tedious analysis. By the best of his estimations, it would not be done until later this evening. He planned on staying at work until the program concluded.

I wonder where Ronnie really is, or if he is even still alive? The only thing they ever found out was that the person he'd left with was named Derek Patterson. Derek had a bad reputation for violence and had been arrested on more than one occasion for beating up hookers.

Larry's cell phone chimed. He looked at the number, and it came up as unknown. He almost deleted the text that accompanied the chime until he realised that it was from Ronnie.

"I need to see you. Can we meet at Dooley's? My life is in danger. —Ronnie."

"I'm on my way. Should be there in ten minutes."

"OK."

To hear from Ronnie was startling enough, but the terse context of the message originating from a strange cell phone number unnerved Larry.

A few minutes later, Larry was in Dooley's, sitting on a stool next to the door. Megan greeted him and served him his usual Guinness, but he was much too nervous to even pick up the glass.

Megan sensed that something was badly amiss. "What is it, Larry? You look like you've seen a ghost."

"Almost. I heard from a ghost. Ronnie just texted me and said that he was going to meet me here in a few minutes—and that his life was in danger."

By then, Big John had joined the conversation. "Didn't Ronnie disappear about a year ago?"

"He did, and we have heard nothing from him since that time. I was afraid he was dead. None of us ever heard from him again, and the police are of absolutely no help at all," explained Larry.

A full forty-five minutes had elapsed since Larry had heard from Ronnie. His concern now escalated to outright anxiety. Then Ronnie, or at least someone who remotely resembled him, stumbled through the front door, almost collapsing as Big John rushed around the bar to help him stand up.

Ronnie's clothing was in shreds. His dirty, matted hair looked like it had been chopped off. His face was filthy and gaunt. His body was totally wasted, and he could not weigh more than one hundred pounds. In short, he looked like death warmed over.

Big John and Larry simultaneously gasped. Larry said, "My god. Ronnie, what has happened to you?"

"I got away, but I'm sure Derek is after me. He threatened to kill me if I tried to escape."

Megan and John held him up by his arms and led him to a corner booth. Megan tried to get his matted hair out of his face, and she had a wet napkin that she was using to clean some of the most obvious dirt off of him. He smelled awful, for which he profusely apologised, stating that he had been allowed access to only enough water to drink. John brought out a hamburger and fries, which Ronnie ravenously devoured. "I was only given one meal a day, and it was mostly stuff that looked and tasted like dog food. I went through almost a month of severe steroid withdrawal. Many times I thought I was going to die, and I actually hoped that I would rather than endure Derek's abuse and torture.

"When we left here that evening, we stopped by another bar and had a few more drinks. By the time we got to his house, I was having a hard time walking. We had no more gotten in the house than Derek hit me in the face and pushed me into a small, windowless room with only an iron bed and an orange Home Depot bucket, which had to serve as my toilet. Derek put an ankle chain on me and chained me to a big iron bed. He had a long, ugly knife and told me that if I did not do everything he ordered, he would cut me up slowly. If I didn't please him, he would kill me and dispose of my body, and no one would ever find me. He indicated that he had done that before. I was absolutely terrified."

"He would beat me for no reason and raped me on an average of two or three times a day. He would always push me over the end of the bed. Fortunately he usually got done very quickly and would leave, but he always came back. He always held his knife against me while he was raping me, and many times he would cut the skin and use his finger, dipped in my blood, to write obscenities on me. He called me his whore and said that he owned me and he would just as soon kill me because I could be easily replaced."

"How did you get away?" asked John.

"There was a metal piece of the bed frame that was loose on one end. I bent it back-and-forth for months until it finally came loose. I hid it under the mattress, waiting for my chance. This morning, when Derek brought my food and set it on the bed, he turned his back on me to pick up the bucket. I honestly don't know where I found the courage, but I pulled the piece of steel from under the mattress and smashed it against the side of his head as hard as I could. He went down, but I'm certain he didn't stay down very long. I was absolutely frantic because I was not even certain that he would have the key to the leg iron with him. I had observed a large key ring on his belt which had a lot of keys on it, and I assumed the leg iron key would be there. Thank God that it was. As soon as I got it off my leg, I snapped it around his leg and took the keys with me, but I'm sure that he has gotten loose by now. I took his cell phone, and that is how I called you."

"Should we go to the police?" asked Megan.

"Please, I just want to go someplace safe and rest. Can we see the police tomorrow?" pleaded Ronnie.

Larry replied, "I'll take you back to my place. You should be safe there because I doubt Derek knows where I live. It's very likely that he will show up here looking for you."

No," said Ronnie. "I've gotten you too involved already. It is not safe."

"After you disappeared, and based upon all the problems with gay harassment, I took a police-sponsored self-defence course last year. I have a concealed carry permit, and I always have my loaded pistol with me. I actually have become a very good shot and usually go to the gun range at least twice a month to stay in practice. Trust me—I can look out for us."

"I'm still scared," said Ronnie.

"I can certainly vouch for Larry's ability," added Big John. "I've seen him shoot at the range, and he is good."

Megan looked surprised. "John, you never told me that."

"You never asked me, and I never really thought it was important," replied John.

"Come on, Larry. Let's get you home, get you cleaned up, and get you in bed so that you can rest."

Soon they were in Larry's apartment, and Larry helped Ronnie into the shower, Ronnie's first one in over a year. As Larry helped him, he could not believe what had happened to Ronnie's body. He was literally skin and bones, weighing at least thirty pounds less than Larry; it was a far cry from his previous 210 pounds of steroid-induced muscles. Larry lathered him down with body wash. While his skin soaked, it took three tries to finally get his hair clean and unmated. Larry tenderly washed him all over.

While cleaning Ronnie in the shower, Larry noted a dramatic improvement in his male functionality. While being washed, in spite of Ronnie's trauma, he began to develop an erection, the first one that Larry had ever seen him achieve. In all the time that Larry had been his lover, his testosterone production had been so steroid suppressed that he was essentially a non-functional eunuch.

"Being off steroids has certainly helped revive your sexual competence," Larry remarked.

"Don't even talk to me about sex. I used to love sex, but now I'm so traumatised by this past year that I'm going to need a lot of time to come to grips with what has happened to me. That felt good, but I am absolutely not ready."

"I'm sorry, Ronnie. I did not mean anything by that. We will take all of the time required to get reacquainted and bring you back to our world. I fully understand how you must feel. We will all help you put this miserable, painful experience in the past. I have missed being with you. You made a bad choice. People make mistakes, and that's how we learn. This absolutely was not your fault."

They lay down together on Larry's bed, wrapped in each other's arms. Ronnie was so exhausted that he was asleep almost instantly. Larry was burning to make love to Ronnie, but he resisted and was content that they were together again. Larry was so keyed up by the day's events that all he could do was lie there and look at the ceiling.

Larry finally realised that the light in the front room was still on. He slipped out of bed, made his way in to the front of the apartment, and switched off the light. He never thought to check the chains and deadbolt on the door. That was something that he did automatically without thinking about it the moment he walked into his apartment, but tonight with the confusion of dealing with Ronnie, he forgot and never returned to the door.

Derek had suspected that Ronnie would seek out his friends, and so rather than trying to track him down, he would go where he thought Ronnie would go: Dooley's. That was exactly what Ronnie had done. Derek had eventually gotten out of the ankle bracelet; Ronnie had not snapped it fully shut. By the time Derek got to Dooley's, Ronnie had already gone inside, and so he waited patiently across the street to see where they would go, his head still throbbing from being struck by Ronnie. *That piece of queer shit will pay for this,* he thought.

Eventually the two of them came out and started walking up the street towards Larry's flat. *Good,* thought Derek. *He doesn't have a car, so it can't be very far to where he lives.* It was easy to follow them unnoticed to Larry's apartment building. The building was an old brownstone style with three stories. By counting the small windows indicating bathrooms, Derek ascertained that there were six apartments on each floor.

By now it was getting dark, and it was easy to remain in the shadows and observe. Derek watched them go through the front door, using a conventional key to open it. Very good. He hated keypads and card keys; they were much harder to defeat. Shortly thereafter, lights came on in the third-floor right front apartment. He crossed the street, and a quick look at the front door revealed an old-style lock that was easily defeated by his knife, which he inserted between the doorframe and the door, pushing back the bolt and giving him immediate access to the front entryway. He took a quick look at the mailboxes, and although he did not recognise Larry's name, he determined 301 should be the front apartment, which would match with where he saw the lights. *This is way too easy,* he thought, grinning to himself as he pictured what he planned to do to the two of them once he was in their apartment.

He made his way up the stairs and down the hall until he was in front of 301. There was light coming under the door, and he could hear a shower running and the sound of people talking. "Even better. I will wait until they get in bed. I hope they are having sex. That would make it even more fun. After I'm done with them, this will be just another unsolved gay murder to which the police will devote minimal attention." He waited in the shadows at the far end of the hall; no other tenants came or went.

Derek waited about thirty minutes and went back to the apartment door. The light was still on, but he could not hear any voices. *I will give them a little more time,* he thought. *Surprise them in bed.*

He retreated back to the far end of the hall, sat in the shadows on the windowsill, and watched. He was very good at waiting and watching; it was something that he had perfected. Patience and then surprise was how he had collected some other interesting specimens over the years, and so far he had never been caught.

He finally returned to the apartment door. The light was out, and there was no sound coming from the apartment. He used his knife to defeat the old-fashioned key lock, turned the knob, and very slowly pushed on the door, expecting to run into either a chain or deadbolt. Neither obstructed his path. *More good luck*, he thought. There was very little light in the apartment. What light there was made its way in through the front blinds from the street light. He moved slowly and cautiously in the dark towards what he assumed to be the bedroom.

A sound from the kitchen area startled him, and he moved a little too fast and bumped into a low coffee table, knocking something off of the table. It fell with a muffled thump onto the carpet. *Shit—I did not see that table.* The sound was the refrigerator starting, and he hoped if they were still awake, they would associate these sounds together. He held his breath, but the apartment was totally silent except for the low hum of the refrigerator. No sound came from the bedroom, and no one turned on a light. Derek felt confident that the element of surprise was still on his side.

Larry had not yet fallen asleep. He was still working through the events of the day and trying to make sense of all of it. He heard the sound of the vase falling on the carpet. He knew exactly what caused that sound because he had run into the same table in the dark in the past, knocking the same vase onto the carpet.

He must have followed us, and now he in my apartment. Damn, I just realised I forgot to chain and bolt the door.

Larry reached up under his pillow and retrieved his Berretta M9 automatic. He quietly moved it down under the covers, holding it by his side in his right hand, essentially aiming it at the open doorway. He silently released the safety.

What did my instructor say? If your life is being threatened, then you are justified in neutralising that threat by any means possible. If you aim your weapon at someone, you need to be ready to pull the trigger. If you pull the trigger, make it count—three body shots minimum. OK, I can do it if I have to.

Larry waited in silence. *Jesus, how many sounds you can hear when you are on full alert?* The refrigerator was running, his cell phone charger was emitting a high-frequency whine, and other miscellaneous night sounds could be distinguished.

Without making any noise, but fully expected at this point, a large man appeared, silhouetted in the opening of the bedroom door and backlit by the street light coming through the front windows. He stood there very still and very quiet for an impossibly long time. Larry was equally still and quiet, but with his gun trained directly on where he anticipated the man would move. He did exactly what Larry had assumed he would do, quietly moving into the bedroom, stopping at the foot of the bed, and continuing to observe what he thought were two sleeping people.

Derek backed up slightly, reached to the side, turned on the bedroom light, and was back at the foot of the bed in an instant, his knife in his hand. He grabbed the foot of the covers. "OK, queers, get ready for some surgery!" He ripped the blanket off of the two figures in the bed.

The last thing that Derek saw was the muzzle flash as three 9 mm slugs tapped a tight pattern across his chest. Later, according to the ME report, two of the bullets passed through the heart, and the third passed through the adjacent lung. The shots to the heart caused immediate cessation of blood pressure and consequently blood flow to the brain, which dropped to zero in 1.2 seconds. With no blood flow, the brain loses vital oxygen, and within 3.5 seconds it basically stops functioning. It is estimated from guillotine executions in the 1700s in France that visual perception may last as long as 6 seconds until all level of awareness ceases. The police report stated that death was instantaneous; technically, he was dead before he hit the floor. What Derek felt and saw in those last few seconds, no one can conjecture with any certainty. Whatever Derek felt or saw, Larry felt no remorse; the bastard deserved that and much worse.

Ronnie screamed and cowered beside the bed. Larry sat there looking at the gun in his hand, with Derek losing a lot of blood on the floor. Still shaking, Larry picked up his cell phone and called 911. He then immediately called Big John and explained what had happened. John called Nedra Wiggins, who arranged for one of her attorneys, James Rowe, to meet them at the police station.

In almost record time, the apartment was flooded with police officers, the county coroner from the medical examiner's office, multiple detectives, and of course the always-present news media, trying to make much more out of this than it really was.

The lead police detective turned out to be Larry's self-defence instructor, who promptly declared that this was obviously self-defence and a justifiable homicide; he did not recommend any charges be filled. "You will need to go down to the station to file the required paperwork, but I do not see any reason to press charges against you," he advised Larry.

Ronnie was still wrapped in a terry cloth bathrobe, huddling on the couch, when Megan arrived. She spent the next few minutes sitting beside Ronnie holding his shaking hands.

"This has to have been a nightmare. It cannot have happened," Ronnie sniffed.

"It was a nightmare, but it is all over now," said Big John. "Thank God that Larry took that self-defence course, or there would be two different bodies to identify."

Derek was former military and worked as director of security at a large import-export warehouse complex in South Portland. He was never married and was a self-proclaimed loner. As a result of his death and a subsequent search of his apartment, three other cold case knife murders of gay men, one dating back fifteen years, were solved. The knife made a very distinctive wound pattern, which linked Derek directly to these cases. A thorough search of his home revealed a massive catch of homosexual pornographic material and many flash drives with digital photographs of men being held captive in that back room. Ronnie was not the first person to occupy the room as a sex prisoner, but with Derek dead, the entire story may never be known. A full excavation of the backyard of Derek's home was planned as soon as the appropriate paperwork was approved.

The psychiatrist in the medical examiner's office declared that Derek was a repressed homosexual, never admitting this preference but acting out his defence of his own inner feelings by blaming the need for homosexual contact on his victims.

One week later Larry, Ronnie, Sherrill, and Cheryl were sitting at a back table in Dooley's and recounting last week's adventure. They went over everything that had happened to them. Ronnie's hair was now back to its accustomed blond, trimmed shorter to accommodate all of the damage. He still had numerous bruises but was beginning to heal, and he had already put on two pounds. He had sworn off all bodybuilding chemicals and all drug use.

Larry's DNA analysis program had made it through its first successful run, and the project director was already declaring the program to be a brilliant breakthrough in progressive DNA analysis. He was still one elusive double-digit lottery number away from the big payoff.

Conclusion

This chapter requires tackling the stigmas of homosexuality and lesbianism, or as it is more politically correctly stated today, gay individuals. We talked about the morality of same-sex interplay in chapter 3, so there is little need to repeat it here. The important message to be learned is that same-sex couples can truly love each other and carry this love and bond as deeply as the more "conventional" opposite-sex marriages. Ronnie and Larry did not fully realise the commitment to each other until Ronnie's life-altering event, where both of them faced imminent mortality at the hands of the deranged Derek. In life, it often takes some major event to allow individuals to more clearly see and understand the depth of their relationship with others.

Questions

1) Compare the relationships of Larry and Ronnie and Ronnie and Derek. Do you think both relationships are realistically portrayed?
2) This is the only one of these stories in which not every participant is a willing participant. What other non-consenting situations can you think of? How can a person guard against unwanted encounters?
3) How do you feel about Larry's reaction to Ronnie's return? Do you think it is realistic?
4) Was Larry morally right in shooting Derek? What other action might he have taken?

CHAPTER 8

RESURRECTION

It had been just over six weeks since Ronnie's miraculous escape from hell. He still could not bring himself to even think of sex. The anus and rectum are very resilient organs, but repeated forced rectal penetration is intensely painful and can sometimes result in tearing of the rectal sphincter, resulting in long-term scarring and incontinence. Ronnie had been seen by two different specialty physicians, each of whom had given him essentially the same answer: he had suffered no permanent damage from Derek's repeated assaults upon him. Yet the memories were so vivid and violent, combined with starvation and beating, that he found it impossible to lower his guard even with his closest friends.

Tonight he sat in Dooley's at their favourite table with Larry, Sherrill, and Cheryl. All of them were glad that it was over. They were together again, and they were all right. Ronnie was beginning to feel better. He'd put on considerable weight, was eating well, had his hair and nails repaired, and proudly wore a new outfit. But he still had no intention of going out to party. He was staying in seclusion at Larry's apartment, only venturing out to meet with his closest friends at Dooley's.

Larry had been very patient and considerate of Ronnie's feelings.

Cheryl, often direct and to the point, finally brought up the subject. "So, Ronnie, are you're ever going to consider sex again?" A moment of total silence from the other three at the table followed this bold and to-the-point question.

"I really don't know," Ronnie finally replied. "Those thirteen months were so brutal and traumatic that I don't know if I could ever possibly enjoy sex again."

"Sure you can," said Cheryl. "Remember about three years ago when I was abducted just around the corner from here? That miserable piece of shit hit me up the side of my head, dragged my unconscious body back behind a dumpster, and repeatedly raped me vaginally and anally. As a finale, he pushed a filthy beer bottle up my vagina and left me there for many hours until you all finally found me, bleeding and still unconscious. That episode landed me in the hospital for major repair work. I got over that. You can get over what happened to you."

"We were all there for you, Cheryl," said Sherrill. "And we're all here for you, Ronnie."

"I don't know. I'm scared to relive the experience."

"You will not relive the pain and torture. We are your closest friends, and we know how to make you feel good again," said Larry.

They all held hands and looked at Ronnie.

"OK, I have to face it sometime. You are right; I can put it behind me."

"Let's go to our apartment," said Cheryl. "Then we can discuss who will do what to whom and how many times, just like the old days."

They all had a good laugh, paid the bar tab, and left Dooley's hand in hand.

Cheryl and Sherrill had a huge, well-appointed apartment. Both women had extremely good jobs, and their combined incomes allowed them a very pleasant lifestyle.

"The first order of business is comfort and relaxation" said Cheryl as she poured four glasses of Duck Horn 2013 Sauvignon Blanche. They saluted their combined good fortune to have such loyal friends. Both women flanked Ronnie and stroked and rubbed his arms, back, and legs. Larry was content to watch their expert massaging of Ronnie, who was rapidly relaxing and basking in the physical attention.

"Two glasses of good wine, and now we need the final relaxation of a hot shower," suggested Cheryl.

Clothing was shed, and all four got into the big glass and marble shower stall. Cheryl and Sherrill were quite similar in appearance and often even dressed the same. They both had short blonde hair and very pretty features complemented by great bodies. There the similarities ended. Sherrill was a believer in no body hair, being perfectly shaved everywhere. She had a clitoral ring piercing, and her small firm breasts were accented with nipple rings. Cheryl, on the other hand, was adorned with a luxurious auburn bush, large breasts, and no piercings.

Hot water and a liberal application of body wash soon had all four of them beyond relaxed and rapidly reaching a plateau of erotic excitement, including Ronnie, who was now capable of a very respectable erection, which both women were gently encouraging. They towelled off, and both men were directed to lie on the big king-sized bed.

Sherrill lay next to Larry, and Cheryl was beside Ronnie. Both women simultaneously zeroed in on each man's genitalia and proceeded to caress and stimulate the now fully erect organs.

Sherrill reached across Larry and expertly slipped two fingers into Cheryl's exposed pelvis, exciting a cry of pleasure from her. However, she was not distracted from matters at hand.

"I love being bisexual," said Cheryl. "No matter what you do, it feels so good," she giggled.

Both men groaned in full agreement as Larry caressed Cheryl's breasts, and Ronnie passively succumbed to the almost forgotten pleasure of his erect organ being placed firmly inside of a vagina. Sherrill straddled him and impaled his organ deeply into her pelvis. Cheryl smoothly moved on top of Larry, settling herself down on him. Now both girls were "riding the bull", both of them working in tandem with two very willing male subjects.

"I just love being bisexual," restated Cheryl.

"I do too, but I just love the taste of pussy," responded Sherrill.

The four them could not hold back the laughter.

"Semen isn't all that bad either," retorted Ronnie. His comment was a welcome surprise to all of them.

Both women climaxed at almost the same time, immediately followed by both Larry and Ronnie, who could not hold back any longer.

"Dibs on Cheryl's pussy," said Ronnie, and he rolled over and buried his face in Cheryl's pelvis, savouring Larry's substantial contribution to the already very wet area.

Larry followed Ronnie's lead, closing his mouth over Sherrill's vagina and sucking as much of the milky fluid out of her as he could.

This exceeded the tolerance of both women who again revelled in another extended round of simultaneous orgasms.

"What could be better than this?" said Ronnie. "Thank all of you for resurrecting me from a living hell."

"Larry, let's show the girls what men like to do to men." He raised his willing butt into the air, inviting Larry to participate with the assistance of two beautiful women.

Conclusion

The addition of an opposite-sex, same-sex couple in the form of Cheryl and Sherrill adds a more fulfilling dimension to the lives of all four of these individuals. They learn to share their preferential sexual pleasures of same sex, and they realise that, properly presented, opposite sexual pleasures can be equally as rewarding. This only strengthens the argument that human sexuality can easily pass back and forth across the grey boundary between same-sex and opposite-sex attractions.

Questions

1) Do you think that Ronnie would ever have recovered his usual sexual activities without the help of Sherrill and Cheryl?
2) What is one word that best describes the group's approach to helping Ronnie heal?

CHAPTER 9

HAPPY BIRTHDAY

The time was the fall of 1980, when kids still went to the movie theatre, notes were written on real paper, and "good" girls were placed under the strictest of regulations regarding any sexual misconduct with boys.

John Dooley, son of Sam Dooley, the owner of Dooley's Irish pub, was about to turn eighteen. He had graduated from high school in May and continued to debate between going to college or pursuing his dream of working full-time with his father at Dooley's, a business that he would ultimately inherit. Throughout high school, he had been an excellent athlete and a good student, but distressingly, at the age of seventeen he was still a virgin. He and his friends would recite stories, perhaps some real but most embellishments of minor events related to dreamed-of sexual conquests of the available crop of females in their high school class. John had no doubt that some of the stories of sexual exploits with a few of the known willing girls were probably quite true. So far, he was batting zero in this league. The mating techniques of the average seventeen-year-old male were poor at the very best, and he felt that he was at the bottom of the class.

The group psychology of penile size comparisons can either elevate a teenage boy's status or degrade him beyond humiliation in the locker room shower. John always accepted things as they were and was pleased to have a reasonable crop of hair and a substantial growth of what was commonly referred to as the third leg.

John and one of his friends, Luigi, constantly harassed each other in the shower. With John's light Irish complexion, red hair was not as obvious as the mat of black fur on Luigi Delgado, who clearly was growing enough body hair, combined with a short, muscular frame, to resemble a more primitive species of Homo sapiens. Luigi was built like a fireplug and was almost impossible to knock down on the football field. As such, he was a hero on the field and a source of great envy in the showers. He commonly harassed John, asking him if he was ever going to grow any hair. John's casual reply to him was, "I spent my energy growing something more important than a bunch of hair," making reference to the fact that his member was significantly longer than Luigi's.

The true peak of the envy ladder in the locker room was Ralph Johnson, a senior and a classmate of John's. He was the uncontested winter of the "longest dick in the shower" contest. He often achieved a hard-on simply to increase his bragging rights. It was rumoured, and possibly true, that Ralph had successfully seduced all of the easy girls and was now working on some of the more difficult ones.

John was glad that high school was finally over. As soon as he turned eighteen, he could dedicate his time to working in his father's pub. He had been working there since he was old enough to carry a tray, bussing the tables and sweeping the floor, but he could not legally work behind the bar until he was eighteen. John had an even better memory for people than his father. He could remember every customer who had ever come into the bar, and if they were even remotely regular visitors, he would know everything that was openly available—and eventually quite a few of the darker secrets about each of them.

Mildred Bowers, a thirty-two-year-old RN who worked at the local hospital, was a regular two or three nights a week. Mildred had been married one time to a man whom she frequently referred to as a total asshole. They were divorced after five unsuccessful years of marriage, and blessedly they had no children. She stated that she had sworn off any permanent connection with any man after that unsatisfactory union. Mildred was not beautiful, but she would still fall into the category of very desirable, with a great personality, a pretty face, big breasts, and a remarkably good figure.

Sam did not consider Mildred in the class of a hooker, although it was well-known that she had a sizable flock of "regulars" with whom she slept.

The rumour was probably true that many of the better connected males in the Portland city government owed her numerous favours—far better than money. She loved men but was very selective and never expected to be paid. She always espoused the idea that payment for sex degraded a beautiful thing. She always said that she had sex because she liked it, and if a man was unable to properly please her, he never got a second chance.

It was well past nine o'clock in the evening, and only a handful of patrons were left in the pub. Sam was engaged in a deep political discussion with two men at the bar, and John was cleaning up the table area in the back. Mildred had been sitting at the bar for some time. Then she picked up her drink, walked over to where John was working, and sat down at a table.

"John, come sit down and talk to me. I need some company tonight."

"Sure, Mildred." John put his broom and dustpan against the next table and sat down beside her. "What's going on? Slow night?" He laughed.

She playfully slapped him on his arm. "Just never found the right one this evening. Some days are just like that. John you're really a good-looking kid, big for your age with a good body. You're really a nice person. Why don't you have any girlfriends?"

"I really want to go out with girls," said John, "but I never make much progress when I do have a date. Most girls say they don't want to be touched, and some others that I had heard would put out made fun of me for trying."

"In what way do they make fun of you?" asked Mildred in a very concerned, clinical nurse voice. "Can you cite an example?"

"I'm sorry, Mildred. I'm not sure that I can really talk about this to you. I've known you since I was a little kid. I kinda think of you like you are my sister or something."

"Just tell me what happened like you're telling a story about someone else, not you. I have probably heard every story in the book, and unfortunately I have lived many of them. I would bet that I can give you some advice that will help you."

John was still hesitant. "Well, OK. It's embarrassing, but it really was not my fault."

"I'm very sure that it was not your fault, and I bet before we are done, you will believe that as an absolute fact," stated Mildred with emphasis.

"So tell me exactly what happened. Don't spare the details, no matter how embarrassing."

"Last fall, I asked JoAnn—you know, the dark-haired girl who is a cheerleader—out for a movie and burgers. It all went real well upfront, and we held hands as we walked back to her house. She asked me if I wanted to come up on the front porch and sit on the settee for a while; it was still early and she didn't have to go in just yet. Of course I agreed. Her settee is around the corner on a dark side of the porch away from the windows and the front door. It's a real good place to make out, which I had every intention of trying to do."

"Explain to me what you mean by *make out*," Mildred said.

John looked around the bar. *Still enough ambient noise to cover this conversation,* he thought. "Well, you know, make out—like, feel around, do some kissing. Things like that."

"OK, go on. What happened next?"

"I kissed her a few times and then tried to feel her boobs. She didn't seem to mind at first, so I probably squeezed a little bit too hard. She hollered real loud and told me to be more gentle. OK, so I've never had very much experience at all. How was I to know how sensitive those things are? We practiced that for a few minutes. I think I was doing much better at boob squeezing. Then she rubbed the front of my pants, and I damn near jumped off of the seat.

"'My, you are touchy,' she told me. Then she felt it again. Is this too much detail for you?" he asked in all seriousness.

"No," Mildred assured him, trying to keep a straight face. "Keep going." She could feel her panties getting wet just visualising the story.

"OK. So then she let me feel under her skirt all the way up her legs. When I ran into her panties, that really did it—I could feel my dick get really hard. She rubbed my pants some more and unzipped the fly."

Mildred was now rubbing her legs together under the table and was totally into the story. The visuals were getting even better. "OK, go on. What happened next?"

"That's where it really got bad. I was wearing Jockey underwear, and she could not figure out how to get my dick out of my shorts. I tried to help her, but then everything got all tangled up, and I panicked. My dick died right there. The damn thing just went limp and fell over."

"Oh, that is dreadfully embarrassing," said Mildred, who by now had been waiting for the big move at the end of the story, which apparently was not going to happen.

"Even more than dreadful. She laughed at me and said that if I could not do better than that, I shouldn't bother calling her again. 'Only a complete idiot would wear Jockey underwear on a hot date.' She got off of the settee and went into the house, and so far I have avoided seeing her like a plague. Even worse, though, she told some of her friends, and so now I am on a do-not-date list."

"John, learning basic sex is no different than learning how to ride a bicycle or drive a car. You need a teacher and some practice. It is almost impossible to do it right the first time."

"You mean I need to take a class to learn how to fuck?"

"Yep, that's exactly what I mean, but let's refine the terminology. *Fuck* is a vulgar term. In today's vernacular, it is a multiuse word as a noun, pronoun, adjective, verb, preposition, proposition, and a host of other usages, all very crude.

"I prefer calling it the fine art of lovemaking. Yes, it is an art form, and very few men ever take the time to learn the art of how to truly please a woman. This is much more than a single lesson course, but the basics are easy, and beyond that point you can improvise. Every generation thinks they invented sex and the art of love making because sex is so easy. The true art of making love is a compilation of taught and learned personal experiences. In order to eventually get it right, you need to be taught by a master."

"You mean that you would like to give me lessons? No offense, but is this something we should be doing? I mean, with our age difference and everything. You know what I mean?"

"There are many good reasons why we probably should not, but in the very best interest of your future happiness, and the happiness of many young conquests to follow, you need to understand the basics. Only a true master can teach this course." She thought, *Shame on me! Am I a dirty-minded old woman who would just love to devour that young, virgin body? The answer is a solid yes!*

"Isn't your birthday this week?" Mildred inquired.

"I will be eighteen on Friday, June 1, and Dad said that for my birthday celebration, I can work behind the bar at last," John replied with great pride.

"How about I give you a birthday present on Saturday? Stop by my house about eleven o'clock in the morning. I will fix lunch for us, and we will start with some basic clinical coursework. No obligations. If you decide not to do this, just don't stop by, and I will see you around. If all of this turns out to be too much for you, you can leave at any time."

John looked forward to Saturday morning with interest, trepidation, and more than a modicum of outright fear. But the drive of young, unfettered testosterone could override all fear. By the time he reached her door, to say that he was nervous would have been a gross understatement. He was petrified. He had gotten a haircut that morning, taken a shower, trimmed his fingernails, and wore clean clothes. No jockey shorts. He was as ready as he was going to get. He pushed the doorbell button.

Mildred answered the door immediately. She was dressed in a plaid skirt, knee socks, and a tight white cashmere sweater with a pearl necklace. Her long auburn hair was swept back into a ponytail, and she had just enough make up on her face to cover up the early traces of age. She looked like a hot teenage girl.

John's first reaction was total surprise. *Damn, she is gorgeous for an old lady.* But he actually said, "You really do look great, just like we were going out on a date."

"Well, thank you, John. I appreciate the compliment." She ushered him in, and they went into the kitchen and sat at the table. She poured iced tea for both of them and finished working on some sandwiches and chips. "This is just like a date. We don't want to rush anything, and we have all afternoon to practice".

"I have to be at Dooley's by five o'clock. The bar starts to get real busy by then, and Dad says that he needs my help," John said.

"Not a problem," said Mildred. "You will be out of here in plenty of time to get to work. Love is so complex and yet so simple. It is an attractive force between two people that develops into a relationship of trust and bonding. If this does not happen, it was lust, not love. I'm going to show you the difference between making love and being in love. Making love is simple, being in love is when it becomes very complex. Hopefully when the time comes, you'll know the difference."

As they finished their lunch, she continued her lecture. "Your very first move must always be slow and subtle. Never rush or grab anything." She reached across the table and gently held his hands. Then she made one slow sweep up both of his arms and back down to the top of his hands. "Now try that."

John was a quick study. He was soon gently stroking Mildred's arms and hands, with casual contact at first, then more purposeful. Mildred could already feel herself getting aroused.

She said, "Let's go into the living room and sit on the couch. It is a perfect place to start."

They set on the couch side by side. Mildred showed him where to start out with his arms and hands. She demonstrated the technique of properly rubbing gently, usually with the back sides of fingers, across a girl's face and ears and down her neck. "Always slowly and casually, followed by more purposeful caressing if she responds. Some girls like their hair messed with. Others don't. If it's in a tight set, don't mess with it." She released her ponytail, and her long hair fell down around her shoulders. "If it is casual, then they love it. Always go slow and easy." John immediately picked up on this technique and nuzzled her soft, clean hair gently passing his lips and tongue across her ear.

"My god, John, you are a natural! That was a great move, and I didn't even tell you to do it. How about a little bit more, with perhaps some more aggression on the ears and neck?" she suggested.

John was amazed at how soft her hair was and how good it felt across his face. He was also quite aware that he was becoming aroused, but he was trying to ignore it for the moment. Mildred was fully aware of the effect this was having on him, but she too ignored it for the moment. It was too early in the lesson.

She lifted her face up to his and gently touched lips with him, slowly moving from side to side and not stopping.

"Do we get to practice kissing now?" asked John.

"Patience, patience. We are going to get there and much more," she said.

She pressed her lips against John's closed lips and then flicked her tongue back and forth across his lips once to judge his reaction. John truly was a natural. He responded immediately with a tongue probe of his own. Mildred then broke off the connection, sat back on the couch, and continued her lecture. But now she was sure that her panties were not just wet—they were saturated.

"There are three phases of deep kissing—that is, kissing open mouth as opposed to closed lips. Stage one: just a brief check of teeth and the front of her tongue. Don't rush this if she holds back; just gently repeat it the next time you kiss. She will soon warm up and move on to stage two. Here we have what I refer to as duelling tongues. You try to see who can out-tongue the other by moving the attacks back and forth from her mouth to yours. As things heat up, it's amazing what an agile organ the tongue can be. If she responses property and is really aggressive, she will push you on to stage three, which I refer to as deep oral exploration. With this technique, you see how far you can probe, tonsils, pallet, hypopharynx—it depends on how long and how agile your tongue is. Let's do some practicing".

At first, John thought she was going to drown him. He was having difficulty synchronising his breathing with all of the tongue action. He fought back valiantly and finally learned how to time his breathing with the probing. *My god, what an experience,* he thought.

After a moderate amount of practice, John finally proved that he could feel all the way to her hypopharynx, the wall at the back of the throat, but her shorter tongue could not get past his uvula. She even drew a chart on a piece of paper, showing what she was talking about, and then she clearly demonstrated where all of these parts were located. Her nurse's training really came in handy in describing anatomy. She was now actively thinking of the next purpose for that deliciously long, agile tongue.

By now, John was soaking through the front part of his pants. This was not unnoticed by Mildred. She catalogued the thought and moved on. *I'll bet my pants are wetter than his,* she thought.

"The next phase is showing you how you can bring a woman to such a level of desire that she seduces you. That is the true art form." She pushed her chest out to him. "You have been ignoring these things."

"I have not," replied John indignantly. "How can I possibly ignore something that gorgeous? I just didn't think we'd reached that chapter."

"Great answer, and a really good comeback. Start out with just a casual pass and just a little bit of a feel, not much, just to see if she's willing. This is best done while you're kissing and she is already occupied. The trick is to shift the focus smoothly from her mouth to her breasts. By now, not only should she be willing, but she should become the aggressor. Now try it. Remember, caress them gently. Most breasts are tender, and it is only when things really heat up that you can do hard squeezing until it hurts. Then the pain feels good."

She moved her hands over his chest, caressing his muscles, and then instructed him to do the same to her. Her breasts were firm, not enhanced, and very substantial. John kneaded them, caressed, and palpated very carefully under the critical instructions from Mildred.

"This has got to be the greatest course I've ever taken," joked John.

"This is very serious," said Mildred. "I teach many classes in nursing school, and every course has a purpose. The purpose of this course is to give you the confidence and ability to make women happy. In doing so, you will also pleasure yourself in the process. Now let's practice subtly unsnapping a bra."

This required a great deal of practice, dexterity, and coordination, but John finally mastered the casual, one-hand unsnap. *Very cool move,* he thought as Mildred congratulated him on being an excellent student, carefully paying attention to detail and not being distracted—which was better than she was managing to do.

"Now the bra is undone and you have her in the proper mood, but you're still outside the clothing. You want to go for the real thing. She's in the mood, but take it easy. Push your hands up under the now loose front of the bra one side at a time. It is much easier to start with the back of your hands, making it easier to push the bra up. Run your fingers over her nipples, but don't pinch them yet. Repeat this manoeuvre until you have the breasts free and her bra pushed up.

"At this point, kissing is now not only permitted but is required. Again, the word is gentle. The nipples are very sensitive. Licking and gentle sucking are the best techniques. Alternate sides, and don't spend too much time on one or the other."

John dutifully followed the instructions, dramatically heightening the arousal of both of them.

"The next move will be to gently lay her back either against the seat, door, or whatever else is convenient and begin to move your kissing down to her belly. Until you know her much better, this is about as low as you should go." John was breathing heavily as he did as directed. He was now very much aware that Mildred was not only breathing heavily, she was really hot and sweating.

She then took his hand, pushed her skirt up, and pressed his hand against her wet pelvis. "That is what you want to feel. She is really ready for you now." John had never been this far before, and he wanted to spend more time here, but Mildred was intent on moving the lesson forward. "Now we need to work on the technique of getting inside the panties. Most panties are loose enough that you can push them to the side. For the first time, don't ever try to get her panties off. This could be very awkward and possibly a deal breaker. Remember your episode with the jockey shorts."

Mildred took his fingers and showed him how to find the loose area along the groin, then how to slide his fingers down the inside of her panties directly into her wet and eager vagina. Mildred cried out as his fingers slipped inside, and he inadvertently pulled out and jumped back.

"Did I hurt you?" he said with all sincerity.

"No, that was just a cry of pleasure. You can't imagine how good that feels. I'm going to have to help you work on this technique some more, and I may get a little noisy and short of breath, but trust me, I will be OK."

She placed two of John's fingers, then three fingers, deep into her pelvis and showed him how to move them just right. After no more than thirty seconds of stimulation, she experienced her first orgasm of the lesson. She was struggling with John's concern at this point, but she would not let him stop. She pushed his hand deeper and experienced two more orgasms in short order. Then she relaxed her grip on him and allowed him to take his hand out. She lay back and looked at John.

"Congratulations. You just caused me to have three orgasms in a row 'I came three times' is the usual term. You are probably unaware of this, but girls can do this many times. A man needs to know and time himself to accommodate her needs. This separates a quick 'poke and come' from good, meaningful sex. As you heard, it can get pretty noisy, and the woman can get very excited if she is properly stimulated. Contrary to popular male belief, women really do enjoy sex.

"As ready as you are right now, I could give you a great handjob, but I want you to have the full lesson. You can practice at home." She laughed.

"Finally! I thought we were never going to get to this part of the lesson," he said as Mildred unzipped his pants and freed the pent-up organ, which rose to full life immediately.

"Boxer shorts. Good move, and I didn't have to remind you. I don't want you to come too soon, so if I get you too close, tell me." She began stroking his erect penis. John immediately put his hand on hers to wait, and she did. "Don't be shy about having the girl slow down a little bit at this point," she instructed.

Satisfied that he was stable for the moment, she produced a condom. "Never be such an insensitive piece of shit that you have sex with a girl without protection. Neither of you wants a pregnancy at this stage." She deftly rolled the rubber ring down over his organ and looked satisfied with her handiwork. John was amazed at how well this lesson was going.

"Now, help me up and over and let me straddle your lap. Keep your dick up and ready," she instructed.

John followed her lead and helped her straddle across his lap. She deftly pulled her panties to the side, and to his total amazement, their parts slipped together perfectly. The unimaginable sensation of pushing up into a soft hot vagina for the first time was a grand experience that John would remember for the rest of his life.

As he pushed full in, Mildred again exploded into another orgasm and got so excited with moving that she temporarily forgot John's level of build-up. He blasted forth in a display of unbridled, orgasmic spasms.

After their heavy breathing subsided, Mildred was breathless but said in a very clinical tone, "That was a mutual orgasm, a technique generally to be used as a finale of the night. Not hurrying right now is extremely important. You are ready to get up and out. She isn't; give her time." They practiced more stage three kissing while still locked together.

"Another very important factor," Mildred explained, "and one that is often overlooked by a careless male, is the disposal of the used condom. It is really bad form to drop it in the trash can, or even to throw it out the car window where you were parked. The best disposal is to flush it down the toilet if one is available. If discrete disposal is not available, roll it up in a tissue and get rid of it later."

They got off of the couch, and John did as instructed, flushing the condom down the toilet.

She said, "Ready for the advanced course now?"

"There is more?" asked an incredulous John.

"Much more. The first order now is to get rid of all the sweat and mess. How about a shower—together?"

"Together? I never took a shower with a girl before."

"You're about to get another lesson. This one is how to properly treat a girl in the shower," she said.

They went into the bedroom. Mildred took off her remaining clothing one piece at a time. John took all of this in. *God, she is gorgeous,* he thought as she freed her breasts from the remains of the bra, dropping her skirt to the floor. Then she dropped her panties, revealing what John had already felt: a luxurious bush at the bottom of a soft white belly.

She began to take off John's clothes one piece at a time, kissing and caressing as she went. John was already erect again, but she gave it only a passing flip. "OK, let's get in the shower. Lots of soap and lather is very important. First, it feels very good to slick up everything, and second, I plan to kiss most every part of your body, and I don't particularly like sweat and unpleasant body odours."

The hot water and plenty of soap helped John to find endless new pleasures in learning the proper technique of sensually washing a woman. *Beats the hell out of a locker room shower. My dick feels bigger than Ralph's.* He proudly stretched it out for Mildred's approval.

"I know what you're thinking, John. I thought a long time before talking myself into this. You have to consider this is only a lesson. Remember the terms we talked about initially. No love. No regrets. And no repeat performances. I am twice your age, and social problems of enormous magnitude could arise if either of us told anyone. We have come too far to stop now, and we cannot undo what we have already done. I cannot overstress how important secrecy is between us about all of this. No one must know, and we should never do this again. This was only a lesson."

"I fully understand, and I do swear to secrecy. Even if we never do this again, I will relive this afternoon many, many times."

Both of them stood in the shower, holding each other lightly. Mildred looked very seriously at John. "It has been a phenomenal afternoon for me also, and one that I will also recall many times in the future. Let's get on to the remaining part of this lesson. This is where I'm going to show you how to lavish pleasure upon a woman to such a serious and dangerous level that you really don't want to try this unless you are ready for some long-term commitment."

They towelled off, and she led him to the bed. "This is very advanced. You may not get here in the real world for some time, but you will need to know what to do when you do achieve this level of intimacy."

She pulled down the bed covers and had him lie in the centre of the big bed. John stretched out, felt the soft bed sheets, and thought, *Dad and Mildred are great friends. I wonder if he has been here before?*

"Yes, he has. That is between him and me, and it's not important just now," she said with a grin. "I was thinking exactly the same thing you were thinking, which is how I knew what you were thinking. There is nothing serious between us. Your dad gets lonely sometimes, and we are good friends. Obviously, I do not plan to tell him about us."

"Good plan. So now what do we do, Teacher?"

"That is a great student attitude. You will like this next lesson." She started kissing his chest and then his abdomen. Finally she targeted his erection, taking it full into her mouth. John's excitement level was rapidly peaking when she released him. "Down, boy, down. Be good," she coaxed him.

"My god, shit, damn, fuck. That was beyond description."

"Don't get used to that. Most girls take years, and some never really learn how to do that correctly. Let's do this slow and easy a few more times, so you can see and feel what I'm doing. Then you can coach a girl, and some will actually listen and learn."

After a few more lessons on proper stroking and sucking, John exploded into a powerful orgasm, which Mildred knew was coming. She held his head firmly in her mouth until he was spent.

"Did I come in your mouth?" he asked incredulously.

"Of course you did." She planted a solid, messy kiss full on his mouth and forced him to flavour what he had just emitted. At first he was repulsed by the idea, but then as the taste blended with her saliva, it was even more sensual, and he felt his erection returning.

"Next lesson," she said. "Remember a while ago, I said to stop at the panty line until later in the relationship. Now we are much later in the relationship, so let's restart at the breasts and work our way down."

John obligingly and studiously caressed, kneaded, kissed, and licked both perfect orbs until she began to push his head down to her belly. He continued kissing and licking his way slowly past the navel and down to her hairline. He stopped at this point and looked up. "What next"?

"Guess," she said as she pushed his face down into her wet pelvis. The heavy musk of her pheromones was combined with the sweet but somewhat acidic fluids that were coming from her vagina, and John catalogued yet another fantastic first experience: eating pussy.

Mildred pushed hard against his head and moaned. John instinctively pushed his tongue deep into her vagina, and the moan became a scream as she again spasmed through another climax. She held his head still for a few moments, breathlessly continuing her instructions. "Always let the girl decide when she is finished coming and ready to resume playing. Now, the final spot to work on ..." She pulled his face up until his mouth was firmly over her clitoris. "At first, only gentle licking and sucking, please," she instructed. After a few minor adjustments to position and pressure, John was able to bring her to an even more intense orgasm, if that was possible.

"Stop! You have to stop. That last one almost ruined me! Well, not really, but you are very close to exceeding my tolerance for one day. We now have only the finale." She rolled another condom across the still erect organ. "Youth is so wasted on young people." She straddled him and inserted him deep into her pelvis. She rocked and undulated repeatedly, taking herself and John almost to climax, and then intuitively slowing down. "You can do this for a long time if you can control everything. Notice how much better control you have already mastered?" The control intervals were getting significantly shorter when she rolled off of him, spread her legs, and said, "This is the finale. Fuck me like you always dreamed you wanted to."

John did exactly as instructed. Tchaikovsky could not have orchestrated it any better. Both had simultaneous powerful orgasms complete with drums, cymbals, and cannon fire. They held each other tightly as their breathing and heart rates gradually returned to normal, and then fell apart, totally exhausted.

"Did I pass?" asked John.

"I would put a gold star on the end of your dick, but it would just slide off," she laughed.

True to their pact, they never talked to anyone about that afternoon, and they never repeated that performance. They remained very close friends throughout her lifetime. John often thought that something that perfect could never be duplicated. The first time truly was the best.

Mildred lived for many more years, finally succumbing to a massive heart attack at the age of seventy-one in July 2014. She had been more than a friend to many of the over one hundred people who attended her funeral. Each man there could look to his neighbour and wonder, with some degree of certainty, whether he was also one of Mildred's "friends". Mildred was always able to segment their special physical love into a small, isolated compartment of time that was theirs alone. She made each man feel very special during that moment.

For a woman who worked as an RN at the local hospital and never charged for her "services", Mildred left an estate valued in the millions of dollars to the benefit of many local and national charities. "Knowledge is worth far more than money," she often told John. "It is amazing what a man will let slip under the right circumstances."

As one would suspect, she was never held in high esteem by the ladies of Portland society, and consequently she had very few declared male friends and almost no female friends. Megan and Nedra were two of her closest friends. Before they were married, John told Megan that he had been one of Mildred's "close friends" as she would have always suspected due to John's friendship with Mildred. Megan always said it was better to know the true story than to guess. Nedra had been Mildred's legal counsel for most of her life, handling her legal and complex business affairs in total confidentiality. Nedra often wondered if Kevin was one of Mildred's "friends". *No way. He is much too professional. Or is he? This might explain his superb understanding of the needs of a woman.* She sent a silent prayer: *Thank you, Mildred.*

Unbeknownst to so many of these fine women of Portland's upper society, Mildred had been the deciding factor in holding together numerous marriages that would have otherwise failed. She had given many of the husbands the insight into the problems which they often shared with her.

Late one evening in Dooley's, just months before she would pass on, Megan asked her, "Mildred, you still look twenty years younger than I know you are, and you still obviously enjoy meeting your friends for a drink and fun. How do you do it?"

"I am still a feisty old lady, and age has absolutely nothing to do with sex. By now, half of my closest male friends can't even get it up with my superb help. This does not stop either of us from enjoying all the other pleasures that can be bestowed upon each other using the systems that still work."

Mildred firmly believed in a type of love that would not work for one man alone. For all her insight and compassion for people, she was never able to build even the beginnings of a monogamous bond. In many ways, however, the bond that she developed with her closest "friends" was a more secure and lasting type of love, even if it was compartmentalised into precious moments of time.

Conclusion

This story illustrates an attraction between an older woman and a younger male who was a mature but totally inexperienced teenager. This is not meant to sanction this type of relationship, but to illustrate that there truly are no boundaries between mutual sexual attractions. There is a fine line between consensual sex and predator sex which often cannot be differentiated, and so this boundary is established by legal terms based entirely upon the age of the younger individual. Conventional thinking looks at the age difference between couples and attempts to pass moral judgement if the span of years exceeds an artificially established acceptable limit. Chronologic age is meaningless in terms of love, as noted in the attraction between Shauna and Robert in chapter 2.

There will be those who argue that the age boundary is a solid line not to be crossed. Mildred rationalised, rightly or wrongly (we cannot judge), that her seduction of John was not a predatory seduction but a giving of herself willingly to him. To this end, she did just that, and in doing so she allowed John to bypass many of the mistakes and unpleasant learning experiences that young adults must go through before reaching full mental sexual maturity, which always occurs much later than physiologic sexual maturity.

Questions

1) Does Mildred have it right? Do you wish you (or the man in your life) had the benefit of Mildred's teaching?
2) Mildred obviously enjoyed this occasion. Was she selfish and taking advantage of a much younger man? Or was she genuinely giving a service?
3) Have you ever had the desire to make love to a younger or older individual?
4) Do you believe that there is an age boundary?

CHAPTER 10

FOUR PLAY

As anticipated, the Clyde Jon case went to trial starting the first week in December. James Glenn Rowe III, lead attorney on the case, had requested that Dr Harvey Johns, the defence's star expert witness, be present during the testimony of the plaintiff's expert witnesses to aid the defence in their case. He would also be the final witness to testify, probably on Friday. Most of the first day was spent in selecting the jury—a job that James took very seriously.

Flights from the West Coast to Portland were miserable even for seasoned flyers in first class: 7.15 a.m. out of LAX connecting in Charlotte, and finally an RJ arriving Portland 8.30 p.m. Monday evening. Dr Johns let James know that he had arrived safely and promptly went to bed.

On Tuesday, the second day of the trial, Dr Johns spent the entire day observing the legal process. He had nothing to do except observe and take notes about anything that seemed significant. He found it difficult to concentrate on the court proceedings because his mind kept drifting to James's wife, Suzanne, and the fantastic time the three of them had had a few months back. And there was the promise of an even better time to come.

To his dismay, testimony took much longer than anticipated, and the last witness wrapped up just before 5.30 p.m. James and the other two attorneys working on the defence's case decided that it would be advisable to continue working that evening preparing Dr Johns' testimony and crosschecking their notes concerning the seated jurors. Dinner was brought in, and they worked well into the evening. No time to play tonight.

Wednesday went much better. The trial moved along at a more intense pace, with one of the plaintiff's expert witnesses being on the stand for over two hours as James grilled and questioned him unmercifully. Then another hour was spent in cross-examination by the plaintiff's attorneys. This was the first time that Harvey had actually sat through an entire trial. It was relatively unusual for an expert witness to be allowed to observe the proceedings outside of his or her specific appearance. As part of the agreement, the plaintiff's expert was also allowed to attend the entire trial, and the plaintiffs' attorney reserved the right to recall his expert for further questioning after Dr Johns' initial testimony.

They finished early and met Suzanne at Dooley's for drinks before dinner. As James and Harvey walked in, they spotted Suzanne in a corner booth with another girl.

Both women got up as the men approached. Suzanne welcomed Harvey with a bear hug, crushing his chest with her solid breasts. She turned and welcomed James with equal enthusiasm.

"Harvey, I'd like to introduce a good friend of ours, Julie Barrett, who is an attorney in James's firm. She is currently based in Boston, but she is in Portland for a few days working on a case. I filled her in on the basic details of our last fun encounter, and knowing her legal thoroughness, I suspect that she has thoroughly vetted you through the firm," she said mockingly.

"That's not fair, Suzanne. Well, actually, I did access his CV, which we have on file. Very impressive, Dr Johns!"

"Please, Julie. I'm sure that we don't need that level of formality. It's just plain Harvey. I hope we will be able to get better acquainted."

"No doubt about that," added Suzanne. They finished their drinks and ordered a second round as plates of the famous Dooley's fish and chips arrived.

"That was so much food that I don't think I can move after that," Harvey remarked, leaning back against the booth and pushing his decimated plate to the centre of the table.

"Yeah, these tight clothes are killing me," interjected Suzanne with an evil smile.

The night was very cold. A land breeze out of the north had dropped the temperatures close to ten degrees with light snow falling. The group was well bundled against the cold, and in anticipation of the evening, they frolicked with linked hands up the centre of the deserted, snow-covered street.

The apartment was warm and cosy. Suzanne had a rack in the front hall for hanging wet outer garments, and they proceeded on into the living room, where James lit the gas logs and opened the drapes that covered the large picture window with a view of downtown Portland. City lights interspersed with Christmas lights as far as they could see, with an overlay of light snow falling; it provided a truly fairyland scene.

"I really miss Portland," Julie said. "Boston is so crowded, and the unbelievably expensive apartment that I live in has windows only in the front room and in the back room, neither with much of a view."

Harvey agreed, standing at the window and now holding Julie's hand. "In order for me to see snow, I have to leave home. That was fun, just walking up here from Dooley's."

"Shower first?" asked Suzanne, and she took James's hand and walked into the bedroom, stripping off her clothes as she went.

Julie quickly took up the cause. After stepping into the bedroom, she slowly removed her blouse and stepped out of her slacks while closely observing Harvey's response. Harvey accepted the challenge and began to methodically remove his clothes, placing them in a neat stack on a nearby loveseat. Julie then removed her bra, revealing small, firm, upturned breasts. She stepped out of her panties, displaying no pubic hair. She was perfectly shaved with a ring piercing visible at the upper edge of her introital cleft.

Harvey stared in wonderment at the two different, but not all that dissimilar, women standing naked in front of him and inviting him to take a shower. *And I can't tell anybody about this! I doubt they would believe it anyhow.*

The four of them got into the shower, and Suzanne adjusted the two showerheads to deliver the perfect amount of water at the right places. She passed out the body wash to the two men and invited them to give them a good rubdown and cleaning.

James and Harvey eagerly took up the task, smoothing the slick soap over each of the women's bodies, foaming and rubbing every part. Julie especially enjoyed Harvey's running his hand down her back, between her buttocks, and emerging in front, rubbing and palpating all the way.

"Doctor, do you examine all of your patients this way?" she laughingly inquired as she obligingly soaped him in precisely the same fashion, pulling his fully erect organ against her belly wall.

"Only the cooperative patients." Harvey was toying with her clitoral ring. "It looks like it should hurt."

"It did for a day or two, but now it just adds another dimension to sensation," explained Julie.

They rinsed off the soap, towelled dry, and made their way to the bedroom.

The two men were instructed to lie on the bed while the women decided what to do to them. The decision was quickly made. Both women started stroking and sucking on the two expanded organs, alternating between the two men. They then switched positions and straddled James's and Harvey's chests, backing up until a female pelvis was in each man's face. Then they assumed the classic sixty-nine position to the total satisfaction of four people moving in perfect synchronization.

Harvey's tongue probed deep into Julie's vagina. He was still wondering about the clitoral ring and carefully avoided it.

Both men were coming very close to orgasm. The women, sensing that moment, released them but continued to push even harder against their faces. Julie climaxed first, followed immediately by Suzanne as they writhed in repeated spasms of delight. Julie and Suzanne then rolled back onto the bed and resumed deep oral kissing.

"They really don't hurt," Julie answered Harvey as he gently teased her nipples with their attached rings. "You can pull on them, and it feels really good." Harvey worked his way down her abdomen to the navel. A small diamond stud was pierced to the skin of the upper side of her navel. This he also investigated with clinical curiosity. "That is strictly decoration," volunteered Julie before Harvey asked the anticipated question. "It does not really add any enhanced sensations."

"Nice. I guess this one can be displayed in public," he joked

Julie pushed his head down farther. "Forget the decorations and check out the practical hardware," she admonished.

Harvey moved his lips over her smooth, shaved pubis and found the next treasure. He clinically examined the placement of the clitoral ring, determining it was through the skin of the hood, the equivalent of a man's foreskin, not penetrating the body of the clitoris. *Much better idea,* he thought.

He gave the ring a few tenuous moves with his tongue, much to Julie's pleasure. She squealed in delight and pressed his face hard against her. Harvey sucked the clitoris, ring, and all into his mouth and used his tongue to manoeuvre everything into correct alignment. He then proceeded to rhythmically suck, thus creating a vacuum over the clitoris, which caused the vestigial organ to swell and experience the equivalent of a male erection. This drove Julie wild, and she instantly had a succession of orgasms, finally forcing his face away from her.

"Stop for a moment. I need some time to recover from that."

With all the noise that Julie was making, Suzanne and James had stopped what they were doing to watch the performance.

"That really looked good, Harvey. How about giving me a lesson? And please show James what you were doing," requested Suzanne.

"It was all just basic physiology," explained Harvey as he went into a dissertation on blood flow and organ engorgement.

"OK, so I get the point. There is a reason why it feels so good. I am eagerly awaiting a clinical demonstration," pleaded Suzanne.

Harvey obliged and eagerly planted his mouth over Suzanne's clitoris. He began the same rhythmic sucking and stroking with his tongue. It only took a few moments until Suzanne was bucking in the throes of repeated orgasms until she also begged for mercy.

James had been carefully observing and wanted to try this technique. Suzanne declared that she was still trying to get her nervous system rearranged. "How about practicing on Julie?"

Julie was very obliging, and under Harvey's careful instructions, James soon became very proficient at this technique, pushing Julie through another series of intense orgasms.

Both women then lay back on the bed, spread their legs wide apart, and declared that that the experience had been absolutely superb.

"OK, I'm assuming that we now need to arrive at some sort of closure, as the politically correct would say," stated James in a very formal, legalistic tone.

They rearranged positions, and neither man could resist the wide-open pelvis spread before him. They assumed the standard missionary position and thrust to full penetration. After a few good, deep pushes, and both women, although reportedly needing a rest, were remarkably revived and added their motion to the rhythm. The men were carefully controlling themselves as both women reached another climax.

Suzanne, always in charge and usually right, said, "This is it. I have one more good one left. You guys take it on the best ride you can." She began to push deep and hard against James.

One cataclysmic, simultaneous, foursome orgasm occurred. Each participant cried out in pleasure. Then all motion stopped. They lay there, melded together, for a few minutes, breathing hard. Then Julie said, "OK, you made the mess, now clean it up." Both women pushed the men off the top of them. They left their legs spread wide apart, and directed the men to their dripping pelvises. This was a challenge that James and Harvey eagerly accepted.

They placed their mouths over the still dripping vaginas and sucked the combination of their own semen mixed with the women's warm and savoury secretions. "An interesting flavour of mixed fluids," stated Harvey in his most scientific voice.

"Let me try some of that," requested Julie, and Harvey obliged her with a mouth full of mixed flavours.

The four of them showered off the sweat and fluids and put on the large terry cloth bathrobes that were hanging behind the towel rack.

"Why don't you guys just stay here tonight? The guestroom bed is not even messed up. We can have a great breakfast in the morning. I make a really mean omelette," said Suzanne.

"That would certainly be fine with me," replied Harvey.

"We don't have to be at the courthouse until ten o'clock," volunteered James.

They all agreed and went to their separate bedrooms. They were too tired and too satisfied for any further play. They continued to hold each other in their arms until they were sound asleep.

Conclusion

The question of morality is often a point of serious consideration in any sexual encounter outside of marriage. We must always consider that morality is a compilation of rules and customs designed by humans. Morality, or lack of it, takes many forms from violence and mayhem through sensual lovemaking. Each component of our life is driven by some sense of morality, both as we see it and as we are taught. It is up to each individual to decide what is morally right for them. Sometimes this will be contrary to laws, regulations, religion, and common sense. In the end, the individual must rationalise whether his or her actions are morally reprehensible or morally acceptable.

This chapter represents consensual lovemaking between four adults for no other purpose than their pleasure and enrichment of sexual experiences. Many of the same lessons from chapter 4 also apply here. James and Suzanne openly and willingly share the sanctity of their marriage with close friends. Who are we to judge the morality of this act of willingly sharing bodies and pleasures with others?

We should never be hesitant to experiment with new techniques of sexual interplay. The old adage is that if it feels good, do it, and if it really feels good, do it again. Nothing could be truer than this when you and your partner have discovered new and often innovative ways of bestowing pleasure upon each other.

Questions

1) Can you believe that this sort of sex play can be fun?
2) Is it realistic to say that Suzanne's husband had no jealous thoughts? Have you ever known a man who would probably react as he does?
3) Do you think that Suzanne and James have agreed that because they are open and sharing in a similar fashion, this counteracts any jealous thoughts?
4) Did the addition of a second female, Julie, change the dynamics from the original encounter as outlined in chapter 4?

5) Is it realistic to consider that Dr Johns could remain emotionally neutral after this series of intimate encounters?
6) Do you think that inviting the same person back on a number of occasions could create conflicting emotional attachments, versus how James and Suzanne have been able to successfully reconcile these encounters in the past?

CHAPTER 11

YESTERDAY, TODAY, AND TOMORROW

Portland Maine, October 1970

Brandon Jordan had been in Portland all week installing the latest version of a revolutionary IBM electronic law practice management program at the Moore, Wiggins, and Short law firm. Dooley's had been recommended to him as a good place to relax after work by one of the partners in the law firm, and he also found out they made a fantastic fish and chips. This would be his last evening to enjoy Dooley's. He had an early morning flight tomorrow out of Portland taking him to Chicago and then home to Springfield, Illinois.

Over the past few days, he had become well acquainted with Samuel Dooley, proprietor and owner of what was touted as the best Irish pub in Portland, and he had no reason to disagree with this claim. After the waitress brought him his evening meal and his second Guinness, he sat at a back booth, continuing to work on wrapping up the paperwork of the installation. He pushed his plate aside, and promptly young John Dooley showed up to clear his table.

"John, I've seen you here almost every evening this week. When do you have time to do your homework?"

"Oh, hi, Mr. Jordan. I work on it between tables. I'm too young to actually come out into the bar, but I can clear tables from this room, which technically is not the bar. I can get a lot of work done in between cleaning tables. Honestly, I don't have that much homework, and it's easy anyway. I just like working in here. Dad says that one day I will own this bar!"

"And with that attitude, I'm sure that you will."

Brandon then went back to studying the printouts from today's test run. *It's passed all of the tests that I can run; I've trained enough people at the firm so that they should be able to load in the remainder of the old data and enter the new data as it comes in. Hopefully the people from training who will be out next week can bring them up to full operating capabilities*, he thought. Installation is a lot easier than training.

He was sorting and cataloguing the data fields printed out on the stack of folded dot matrix printer pages. A powerful sensation of being watched came over him. He looked up over the stack of papers to see a very pretty redhead sitting at an adjacent table, intently watching him.

Their eyes met, and without either saying a word, she got up from her table, picked up her drink, and walked over to the booth where he was sitting. She placed her drink on the table and sat down.

"Hello, Mr Jordan. My name is Christina. I hope you don't take this wrong—I'm not a hooker looking for a pickup. I work across the street and occasionally stop by here for a drink before going home. I noticed you yesterday, and Sam told me what your name was. The first time I saw you, I had this uncanny feeling that I knew you from somewhere or that we had met in the past, but I absolutely don't know how that could be."

Brandon extended his hand to her. "Brandon Jordan. I work for IBM and have been in town all week installing a computer program for a law firm here in Portland. Now that you have joined me, I also feel like I have known you or met you somewhere. Are you from around here?"

"I live up in Falmouth, a town just north of Portland. Born and raised in the area."

"I think I've seen that on the Portland area map. Everything I need is in walking distance, so I didn't rent a car. I have walked around most of downtown Old Portland, but never got out of the area," explained Brandon. Upon noticing her wedding ring, he casually asked, "Married? Kids?"

"No kids as yet. My husband works for one of the local lumber companies and is gone a lot during the week. I'm a salesperson in the dress shop across the street, and so I frequently stop by Dooley's for a drink on the way home. I just like to talk to someone other than the people I work with," she explained. "And you?"

"Married; thirty years old; work for IBM; live in Springfield, Illinois; two young kids," typical brief explanation by a man.

"As I'm sure most people always say," explained Brandon. "Just so you know, I never solicit women at a bar."

Christina replied, "And I was not looking for you or anyone else as a pickup. I love my husband. He has a good job, and I have absolutely no idea why I have this phenomenal attraction towards you." She leaned over and lightly kissed him on the lips.

Brandon made no move to resist. He took both of her hands, looked her straight in the face, and kissed her back lightly.

Brandon folded up his work and slipped it in his briefcase, and they sat there for over an hour, talking as though they had known each other all their lives and were simply catching up on old times. They quickly found themselves relating to what they always attributed to past-life experiences. Both of them subscribed to one of the oldest religious beliefs: that most of us have been here many times before in many previous lifetimes. We often carry forward memories, talents, and associations from these lifetimes into our present existence. And just as surely, we will carry these experiences and associations into the future. They were both certain that they must have known each other in a previous lifetime.

"All of this must have caused the intense attractive force that I felt when I first saw you yesterday. Today it was much stronger, and I had no choice but to talk to you. John told me that you would be leaving tomorrow, and I knew I could not allow you to walk away from a feeling of attraction that was this powerful," explained Christina.

"I only met you a few hours ago, and yet in just this short period of time, it is astounding how much we seem to have in common," he replied. "If you have time, would you like to walk around the area? The wharf looking out across the bay is beautiful this time of night."

"Wherever you want to go. I just feel like I need to spend more time with you this evening."

Brandon paid the bar tab, and they strolled out of Dooley's and headed down toward the wharf area. The evening was unseasonably warm, and quite a few people were still laughing, talking, and moving up and down both sides of the cobblestone street.

They both noticed her at the same time: an older woman sitting at a small card table beside the front door of a shop with a sign proclaiming that it sold candles, incense, and items of mystic interest.

Christina approached her and asked, "Are you a fortune teller?"

"No, young lady, I am not a fortune teller. I prefer to think of myself as a mystic. I could sense you coming to me as soon as you entered the street. Both you and your newly found friend have intense auras surrounding you. If you would like, I can tell you about your past and perhaps something about your future." She said it with great solemnity.

"I feel like this is something I absolutely have to do," said Christina as she sat down at the table.

The mystic lady slowly and methodically shuffled a large deck of tarot cards, finally handing the deck to Christina. "Draw five cards and place them face down on the table." Christina did as she was instructed. The mystic lady took the cards, moved them around on the table a few times, and then arranged them in a three, two pattern. After placing her fingers on all five cards she was silent for a moment. Then she looked at Christina. "You are married, and your friend is married. You have only met in this world this evening, and you wonder why this is happening. You have been drawn to this place, specifically to me, for those answers."

Christina looked up at Brandon in amazement.

The mystic lady continued. "There are so many things that are almost impossible to understand or comprehend. There are those who believe we exist in parallel universes, where time and physical position have no measurements. Both of you have met in the past, in previous lives. You have been family, enemies, and lovers. Today is but one more of those crossing points. It will be short and intense but lasting. You will always remember what happened here. Somewhere, there is a deep reason why you met today. The past is always easier to visualise than the future. It may take many years, but this reason will eventually be revealed to you."

She turned over the first card. "This is symbolic of love, a different type of love than we normally consider. A love that you two will decide upon later."

She turned the second card. "Time is not on your side, but it will be a friend to both of you far into the future. I see distinctly separate pathways for many years, possibly the remainder of this earthly lifetime."

She turned the third card. "This looks deeply into your past lives and verifies what I was originally feeling. You have known your young friend here many times in the past, and you will meet again in the future."

She turned the fourth card. "I see children in your future, and I see that you will be married a number of times before you find the right person."

She turned the fifth card. "I see tragedy, discontent, and death surrounding both you and your young friend. I cannot clarify who or when, but the cards indicate with certainly that you manage to survive for many years, far longer than I can accurately see. That is all these cards can tell you."

The mystic lady looked at Brandon. "All right, young man. You have come this far. You have never had anyone look into your past or future. You were directed to me this evening for a very specific reason. Now you want to know why."

Brandon, having played cards long enough, never played the deck directly from the dealer. He took the deck as directed but reshuffled it three times, cut it twice, and fanned the cards on the table. Without any hesitation, he picked five random cards out of the fan, closed up the deck, and handed it back to the mystic lady along with the five selected cards.

She smiled at him and placed the five cards on the table face down in the same three, two pattern and held her trembling fingers on the cards for many minutes. "The images that I am seeing and the thoughts that I am feeling are extremely powerful. There are many messages to be delivered, and many of them directly affect both of you."

She turned over card one, the same card as Christina's. "This is the same card you just observed: symbolic of love, a different type of love than we normally consider. You will look upon love differently than your lady friend. The message that I feel from this card is that a more intense love will come to you much later."

She turned over card two, the same card as Christina's. "This is very powerful and very meaningful that the two of you have selected the same second card. The message remains the same: time is not on your side, but it will be a friend to both of you far into the future. I see both of you taking distinctly separate pathways for many years, possibly the remainder of this earthly lifetime."

She turned over card three, also the same card as Christina's. The mystic lady gave a look of surprise, and deep concern crossed her wrinkled face. "The chances of a third card being identical and in the same sequence indicates to me that this message cannot be ignored. I can look past you, deeply into your past lives, and verify what I was originally feeling. You have known your new lady friend here many times in the past, and you will meet again in the future. This meeting, at this time and this place, is for a special purpose, but one that I cannot clearly see. It will be many years before either of you will understand the significance of this crossing in time."

She turned the fourth card. This was the first card that was different from Christina's choice. The mystic lady looked puzzled as she studied the fourth card. "I see a lifetime of achievement, rewards, accolades, and a very successful but unfulfilled life. Your influence over others will be enormous. You will be responsible for many changes in your lifetime. You will continually seek for some unknown value or meaning. Your journey in this life is to achieve this goal of understanding, but it may never be fully revealed to you in this lifetime."

She turned over card five, and it was the same as Christina's fifth card. The mystic lady said absolutely nothing as she looked at the card. Brandon and Christina recognised it as the same card in the same sequence. Finally she spoke. "The presence that I am feeling at this moment is stronger than I have experienced in many years. There is a power and attraction surrounding the two of you that spans millennia of time. Your meeting tonight will have far-reaching influences on the lives of many people in the future. I see tragedy, discontent, and death surrounding you and your young friend. I cannot clarify who or when, but certainly you also manage to survive for many years, far longer than I can accurately see. There will be many more lifetimes ahead."

They paid the mystic lady, who immediately folded her table and went into her shop and turned off the lights. They walked on down the street, a lot of unanswered questions drifting between the two of them. They walked out onto an older section of the wharf where they could look out across a few small boats tied to the dock to the spit of land on the other side of the harbour. They stood together, leaned on the rail, and looked out across the bay. Sparkling diamonds of lights reflected off of the dark water.

Christina finally broke the silence. "That was certainly spooky. She hit an awful lot of what little we know about each other dead on. The amazing thing was the parallel predictions for both of us into the future. How did she do that?"

Brandon responded, "I never ever experienced anything like that before. In fact, I had never even considered stopping at a fortune teller because I thought they were all a hoax. Just as with you, Christina, she was right on with many of her statements. I saw her shuffle the deck many times. I took the deck, cut it numerous times, and randomly selected the five cards. The first three cards were identical to what you had selected and in the same order; only number four was different. When she turned that fifth card and it was identical to yours, that's when I seriously believed what she was saying. It was quite obvious that she was also visibly moved by the sequence of those cards. I suspect that she too had a unique experience this evening."

Christina turned and looked at Brandon. "I feel that it is impossible to apply any type of logic to what is happening to us, so maybe ignoring all logic and going with what we feel right now is appropriate. I don't have to be any place tonight. My cat is just as happy if I don't come home, and you are going back home tomorrow. I have a totally illogical and non-understandable urge, need, desire—whatever you want to call it—to be with you tonight, to hold you, to make love to you. It may be our first and last time. Is this totally bizarre? Are you scared or offended by my forwardness? Or are you feeling the same attraction that I am?"

"I felt that attraction the moment I looked up and saw you at Dooley's. Yes, oh yes. Whatever the reason, whatever the conflict, whatever the risk, whatever the outcome, I have to be with you tonight."

They walked slowly back up the street, arm in arm, to the new Holiday Inn Hotel. Room 412 was a nice corner room with a king-sized bed and a view over the harbour area. The two of them stood in front of the large window holding hands, unmoving, and saying nothing for many minutes.

Brandon spoke first. "Christina, I met you four hours ago, but it seems as though I *have* known you forever. If what the old mystic lady said was true, then I have known you forever. This entire scenario has taken place so fast that I'm having trouble compiling my thoughts and processing the answers. I don't want to push you into anything that you don't want to do or that you feel uncomfortable with."

"Brandon, anything that happens over the next few hours is something that I am certain neither one of us would be able to prevent tonight or explain to ourselves tomorrow. I'm on such a different plane right now that the concept of right, wrong, and regrets has been suppressed by a need that is so strong that it cannot be resisted."

Brandon held her hands and then pulled her tightly to him. "I really cannot think of or see anyone or anything at this point, except you and an attraction that exceeds all level of conscious reason. Tonight I have no regrets. How I will feel tomorrow will have to wait until tomorrow."

They turned together, embraced, and enjoyed gentle and then more passionate kissing. They separated slightly and slowly and carefully took off each other's clothes until they were standing nude at the foot of a very inviting bed.

The power, passion, and stamina of their lovemaking were beyond anything that either of them had ever experienced. It was quite early in the morning before they drifted off to sleep in each other's arms, totally exhausted.

The front desk of the hotel rang his room phone, waking Brandon at the prearranged time of 7 a.m. to give him time to check out and get to the airport. As Brandon sat on the edge of the bed trying to wake up after the preceding evening, he realised that Christina was no longer in bed. Neither was she in the bathroom. At that point, he found the note lying on the desk top.

Brandon,

I know that you will be leaving this morning, and I felt that it was better to avoid the complexities of a long and emotional goodbye. All I can say is that it was truly the most emotionally intense experience of my life, and it's one that I shall never forget and will treasure forever. If the mystic lady was correct, we will meet again. This I believe with all of my heart and soul. Love is yesterday, today, and tomorrow.

Christina

Brandon had never managed to get her last name, and it was apparent that she wanted to leave it that way. He respected her wishes and did not try to contact her, although she was never far from his thoughts as his life unfolded and the years continued to slowly flow. He often wondered what became of her and how her life progressed. His life had amazingly followed the predictions of the mystic lady.

Yesterday, today, tomorrow. We had yesterday, today can take a long time, and I will wait for tomorrow.

"Today" would take forty-six years.

September 2016

It had been forty-six years since he was last in Portland. That was literally a lifetime ago. He was here as a consultant to MBI, who were working on a revolutionary DNA analysis program. It had been a few months since he had thought of Christina, and then the potential of a contract in Portland crossed his desk. He personally took charge of the project and made certain that the terms were enticing enough that they would win the bid, which his company did.

He took the lead role in integrating the new compilation routine into MBI's existing software. The installation was relatively short, taking most of one day, but then MBI would need many days to test the algorithm before they accepted the new routine. Either he would have to return later, or he could stay in Portland for a few days. He had to stay. He had to know if the mystic lady's predictions would continue to hold true.

He had arrived late on Sunday and spent all day Monday doing the installation and testing. Now all he had to do was wait, and what better place to wait than Dooley's? He had checked earlier in the day and was pleased that Dooley's was still in business and in the same location.

He walked in, proceeded immediately to his old table in the back, sat down, and ordered a Guinness. "Remarkable! Forty-six years later, and it still looks exactly the same."

“Welcome! You’re a new face here, but you walked in like you know the place,” said a cheerful lady whose name tag identified her as Megan.

“Forty-six years ago to be exact,” replied Brandon with a grin.

“My friend, that’s way too long. This first drink is on the house. John will want to meet you. He always likes returning business.”

“John Dooley?” asked Brandon.

“The one and only John Dooley,” replied Megan. “Owner and my husband.” Megan caught John’s eye, and he vacated the bar and came over to the table. “John, this gentleman says it has been forty-six years since he was last here.”

“It’s hard to imagine that anyone could stay away from Dooley’s for forty-six years, but welcome back.”

Brandon shook his hand. “You were about eight years old and cleaning tables. You said someday you would own the place. Looks like that came true.”

John studied him for a moment, diving through the years back to childhood. This table, this person, his phenomenal memory of people and faces searching for a match. “You always had a stack of computer papers you were working on, and sometimes if you were finished with some of them, you would give them to me. I always liked those big sheets of paper. IBM? Johnson? No, Jordan?”

“Outstanding! Absolutely dead on,” said Brandon. “I was here for a week in 1970. I always sat at this table, summarised my day’s work, and had dinner. You were very attentive and immediately cleaned the table as soon as I was done. The last day I was here, I met a young lady named Christina—a really pretty redhead. Never got her last name, and I often wondered what happened to her.”

John looked up toward the door. “Well, Mr Jordan, concern yourself no longer. You can ask her. In fact, it looks like she’s heading straight for us.”

Christina had let her hair turn grey and had put on some weight, but Brandon still instantly recognised her as she walked up to the table. Brandon got up, and they embraced. John and Megan looked at each other, “Guess we need to get back to the other customers and leave you two to do a little catch-up,” said John.

“Somehow, I just knew you would be here this evening. We have so much to talk about," Christina said. They sat down, started talking at the same time, and laughed. Christina continued. "Over the last few months, I have had more and more communications that kept taking me back to 1970. My God, that has been an absolute lifetime! Two children, three marriages, widowed one time, and two divorces. I am now living alone with my dog. And you?"

"Almost everything the mystic lady predicted eventually happened, including tonight. When I got an RFP for this project in Portland, everything lit up. I knew that we would get the bid, I knew that I would be here, and I knew that you would be here."

Megan slipped a Guinness in front of each of them and then turned and headed back to the bar without disturbing them.

Christina said, "I have never had you far from my thoughts. My first marriage to Ralph, the guy who worked for the lumber company, lasted longer than my next two combined. We had two children who are now grown and gone, but they're producing lots of grandchildren for me to spoil.

"Serena is forty-five, has three children, and lives in Boston. She is married to Dr David Parton, who is a radiation oncologist at Massachusetts General Hospital. Serena has had an unbelievably successful career. She is professor and chief of paediatric oncology at Boston Children's Hospital. She is world-famous for her leading research in the treatment of childhood lymphomas."

"Ralph Junior moved to Montana twenty years ago, and I see him and his family about once a year at holidays. I spent two weeks up there one summer a few years back, but that was my only time. Ralph was killed in a logging accident when Ralph Junior was ten years old. A small life insurance policy helped, but Serena was just starting college. In desperation, I went through two very bad marriages. My second divorce was ten years ago, and since then I have had no real social life—in fact, very little life at all. Maybe I was just waiting for you to come back into my life."

She continued. "I have to admit, I followed your career. It was easy to find you when the new computer search programs became available. I know that your children are grown and you have grandchildren. Your career was phenomenally successful, and even though you're technically retired, you're still working. I also read that your wife died quite a few years ago and you never remarried."

"OK," said Brandon, "that takes care of my history very succinctly."

Christina laughed. "Sorry about that," she said, "I guess I was electronically stalking you, never thinking that I would ever see you again until a few weeks ago, when our time together kept replaying in my memory. I cannot explain how I knew you would be here tonight. I haven't been in Dooley's for at least two months. Then I knew that I just had to be here this evening. Let's go to my house. I want to show you where I live, show you pictures of my children, and get to know you again."

Brandon paid the bar tab with a generous tip, and they walked out with their arms around each other.

"That has to be one of the most beautiful and sad stories I've ever heard," said Megan with visible tears in her eyes.

John wrapped his big arms around her, patted her on her protruding belly, and said, "I thank God or whatever power that brought us together. I wish them the same best luck the Irish can bestow upon them."

Christina lived in a modest, older home just south of the downtown area. The section was made up of old but still well-maintained houses. "I usually ride the bus, but we can walk tonight; it's not that far." A short, pleasant walk later, they were at her house. She unlocked the front door. They stepped inside and were immediately greeted by a small, yapping, ankle-biter Chihuahua mixed with something slightly larger. "This is Sugar," said Christina as she picked up the dog so she could check out Brandon. She sniffed his fingers and licked his hand. He rubbed behind her ears, and she was satisfied that he was a friend. She squirmed out of Christina's arms and headed for her bed. "That's probably the last we will hear from her tonight. She always stays up until she's sure I'm safely home."

She gave Brandon a quick tour of the house and introduced him to her children and grandchildren via the large collection of pictures that adorned tables, mantels, and any other flat surface, covering a wide span of years and generations.

"I regret that we never got a picture of the two of us together," she said. "It would have helped the memories. I confess that there are some very good pictures of you online." She retrieved a bottle of white wine from the refrigerator and poured two glasses, and they sat on the living room couch. They held hands and studied each other's much older but still familiar features.

"I have thought about you so many times," Brandon said. "I would find my thoughts drifting back to that night and wondering what you were doing and how the years were treating you. I even developed a computer program that searched the Portland phonebook for everybody named Christina, but obviously without a last name, that was an impossible search. Even if I had found you, I would've never tried to contact you. What we had that night was one special time that occurred for reasons beyond my comprehension. Honestly, I never expected us to see each other again. You remember that the mystic lady was a little vague about how things would end."

"For many of the same reasons, even though I eventually knew your name and a great deal about you, I never tried to contact you. I felt that what we had and what we did was so special that it could never be duplicated. I eventually realised that our meeting served a deep and long-lasting purpose," Christina explained.

Brandon spent a long time looking at the pictures on the mantle, but he kept coming back to Serena. "I feel that I know her, just as I sensed that I knew you. Perhaps from another life?"

"Actually, it was from that night. I know you felt it by just looking at her pictures. Serena is your child. No one ever knew, and she does not know, but you had to know. She was the purpose of our meeting in that crossing of time. That fact I can be certain of. For what reason, God may know; I cannot explain it. You can meet Serena sometime soon; she often comes to see me on weekends," explained Christina.

"From what you have told me about her, I can see that there was truly a much deeper reason for what we did than either of us will ever understand," replied Brandon. He folded his arms around her and looked deep into her sad eyes. "I love you, Christina. I have since that day, and probably many times before that. But certainly I love you today."

They sat in silence for a long time. Brandon took her hands and pulled her to him. He kissed her lightly at first and then deeper, and she responded equally.

"How has your health been?" she asked.

"Three-vessel bypass in 2010, and radiation therapy for cancer of the prostate in 2013. Both seem to be stable as of now. I generally feel good—a little more tired than before all that, but still going strong." He paused. "And you?"

"A few problems we can talk about later," she evasively answered. She then broached the question both had been waiting for all evening. "Would you think it would be OK if we went to bed?"

"I hoped you would ask, but I did not want to push. What we experienced forty-six years ago can never be duplicated. Neither one of us is probably in shape for that anyhow, but we really can try our best. After prostate cancer, men lose a lot of ability, and I have been no exception."

"I don't care. I just want to hold you and love you as much as I can," said Christina. She took his hand, and they went into the bedroom.

Christina gently took off Brandon's shirt and investigated his mid-sternal scar from the bypass surgery. "Feels OK now?"

"Doing fine," he replied. "It took almost a year to get some of the feeling back in my chest. The only feeling I had after the surgery was pain, but all that has completely cleared. My cardiologist says I'm doing great and the vessels are wide open."

He slowly undid her blouse and as soon it was open he could see her right breast was missing.

"Breast cancer two years ago. Mastectomy, chemotherapy, and radiation treatments. It was really rough," she explained. She undid her bra and dropped it to the floor. "You still have one to play with," she joked.

Brandon replied, "At the rate we're losing parts, we'd better get to work before something else quits working or falls off!" He dropped his pants and shorts and lay on the bed. Christina immediately followed, shedding the rest of her clothes.

They held each other for a long time, savouring the closeness and rekindling a bond that truly had never been broken. They kissed gently at first, then with an intensity neither had known for many years.

Brandon moved down to her chest, holding and kissing her left breast and then running his fingers over the smooth scar line and the three little blue tattoo dots from her radiation treatment fields. "Does that hurt?" he asked, very concerned.

"No. In fact, the skin over that whole area is still numb."

He gently kissed the smooth skin and the scar line. He cautiously moved down her belly.

"Lost all my hair with chemotherapy. Some never came back," she explained. "At least I'm in fashion and don't have to shave it."

Brandon rubbed his hand across her smooth vulva and continued to advance his kissing downward. He looked up at her for approval before advancing any farther.

"Please, Brandon, please. No one else ever made love to me that way," she said as she forced his face down to her pelvis.

She was warm and wet, and as his tongue glided past the labial cleft and sank into her vagina, she pushed hard against his face. She continued to respond with more deep pushes until she arched into an orgasm.

"Oh, my God, Brandon. That was the first time in years that I have actually had a real orgasm, but never since I was with you was it that way."

He continued to massage and probe, now concentrating on her clitoris, and he was rewarded with another series of orgasmic spasms. She freed herself from his grip and turned to face his pelvis. She took his semi-rigid organ in her mouth and valiantly worked on it with some success. She found that she could compress the base of the shaft and achieve a decent erection, but it subsided as soon as she released her grip. She continued to love and massage him.

Brandon now had two fingers inserted deeply in her and was also massaging. He pulled her over towards him and again applied all of his oral talents to her pelvis with the same satisfying results as before.

"Brandon, no fair! I'm having all the fun. What can I do for you?"

"Right now, I'm enjoying this as much as if I was buried inside you. Just my feeling your response and imagining what I'm doing is enough for me."

After a few more minutes of intense sensation, Christina insisted that she try again. This time, she combined synchronism of pressure on the base of the shaft, and oral-induced vacuum achieved by vigorous sucking. She had Brandon feeling sensations that he had not known for years. He could not believe it. He felt the tingle in his legs followed by a tightening of his pelvic muscles, and he exploded into of his first orgasm in years. The fluid production was minimal, but the sensation was maximal, and Christina cherished every drop that she could extract.

She and Brandon fell back against the bed, totally overcome by the fantastic sensations that had enveloped both of them. They lay in each other's arms for a long time. Finally Christina asked, "What will now become of us, Brandon?"

"I don't know. This is all new for both of us. Or is it, really?

"I went back to try to find the mystic lady a few days later, to see if I could get any more answers. She was gone, and a souvenir shop was where she had been. The man next door said there had never been a candle shop there. We both saw her, and she predicted our futures to this point—but did she really exist?"

"Perhaps her existence at that time and place related to the reason that we were also at that time and place. She firmly verified what we were feeling and in doing so allowed us to become one for that very short piece of time. Serena and her positive influence over the lives of so many is the justification for that union. What we did worked the last time, so let's just trust our instincts one more time," replied Brandon.

"I have no written future; you have no written future. Maybe at last it has become tomorrow," replied Christina.

For them, "tomorrow" lasted only a few precious months. When Brandon and Christina found each other, she was in failing health, and her oncologist soon diagnosed metastatic cancer in her lungs and liver. It was only a matter of time until her frail body would be ravaged by terminal pain and suffering. She declined any further chemotherapy and was told that radiation treatment was not an option.

Brandon stayed with her to the very end. Three months to the day when they found each other again, Christina had a massive coronary occlusion and died on the way to the hospital.

Following the funeral, Brandon was talking to Serena. They openly cried and held each other for a long time.

Serena looked up at him. "You loved her very much, didn't you? I saw a love between the two of you that cannot be explained by a brief encounter of only three months. Would you please come by Mother's home after the gathering at the church so we can talk further? I know that there are many things that we need to say."

Later, they were sitting in Christina's living room. Her husband and the children had discreetly retreated to another area of the home so that they could be alone.

"You and Mother had a bond that seemed so much more lasting and deeper than can be explained by a chance meeting between two people three months ago."

"Serena, your mother and I had a brief one night affair forty-six years ago, when I was working in Portland on a temporary assignment. Neither of us was able to explain the intense attraction that we felt for each other during that brief encounter. We could make no excuse for what happened, and afterwards we both went our separate ways with no way to contact each other again.

"That night, your mother and I had the strangest experience of our lives when a mystic lady read our past and our future with an uncanny accuracy. Everything that she predicted has now come true," explained Brandon.

Serena looked at him, tears running down her cheeks. "I feel exactly the same bond with you, even though I have known you for only a very short period of time. I felt this attraction the first time I saw you when I came to visit Mother. I now fully understand why I felt that way. I know that you must be my father, but Mother never told me, and I don't know if she ever told you."

"Yes," Brandon said simply as they held each other for a long time. "Love is so fleeting and tenuous, but Christina and I must have closed the circle with you—what you have done with your life, and what you have given to the world in the form of countless children who owe their lives to you. You were our destiny that night. This clearly was meant to be."

Brandon returned to Springfield after Christina's funeral and died three weeks later of unknown causes in his sleep.

Yesterday, today, tomorrow, and forever.

Conclusion

There are so many things in our lives that we attempt to explain, only to discover that there is no rational explanation for them. This story is a common theme, and in its commonality there must be a base causality. There truly are no coincidences. Things happen, people live and die, but each event is based on a preceding set of circumstances; altering any one of them can change the outcome. For most of the circumstances, we either set them in place or possibly even directed them before they occurred. Some circumstances can only be explained by events that were planned long before we had any conceivable control over the outcome. Once the event occurs. it then becomes our responsibility to accept it for what it is because we cannot change it.

In this story, two individuals separated by vastly different life patterns were inexplicably brought together for one brief moment in their existence. They were drawn into a union, controlled by forces beyond their rationalisation; a new life was created, and they were immediately cast apart for practically another lifetime, only to meet again in their final days of this lifespan on earth.

This is a story of a different type of love: a bond that forms from no rational source, glows brightly for only a brief moment, only to be rekindled many years later, but to die again just as quickly as the circle is closed.

Questions

1) Both of these people are married to others. How do you feel about their one-night stand?
2) Should either of them have confessed to their spouses? What about after the daughter was born?
3) Would they have acted as they did if not for the mystic lady? Is that a valid excuse for their actions? Did they need an excuse?
4) Have you ever experienced a situation where even though you knew the outcome could be questionable, you could not resist the need to experience the moment?
5) Have you ever reflected back upon decisions that you made and wondered if the outcome would have been different if you had listened to your heart and not reason?
6) During their later encounter, they each discovered the other had had physical problems that left scars. Do you think they handled these facts well?
7) Do you wish the ending of this story had been different?
8) Can you relate to the theory of previous lifetimes and predestined occurrences as it intertwines in this story?
9) Have you ever been to a fortune teller?

CHAPTER 12

BLACK ON WHITE

It was 4.30 on a very cold, snowy Friday evening in December. Spencer Thomas gazed out of his office window at downtown Portland. Traffic was still moving reasonably well on the main streets, but he knew the road out of town to his home would be snow packed and slick by this time. His Land Rover should have no problem in getting him home.

Spence was a tall Jamaican with fine features, courtesy of his British mother. His family owned the oldest rum distillery on the island of Jamaica. Spence had grown up in an island of wealth surrounded by abject poverty. He was schooled at Oxford with a major in business. He was never interested in the rum business; that was to be his older brother's job. He moved to the United States twelve years ago and joined a brokerage firm in New York City. He loved New York City, but when the offer to head a branch of the firm in Portland opened up last year, he took the opportunity.

He temporarily lived in an apartment downtown until he could decide whether he wanted to stay in Portland. He found that he loved the slower pace of a smaller city and eventually found a beautiful older home in a gated enclave north of Portland with a great view of the Atlantic Ocean. Spence loved the ocean; the plantation-style home that he had grown up in looked out over the sugarcane fields to the Caribbean. This was as close as he was going to get to that in Maine. It was still so much better than his high-rise apartment in Manhattan.

Martha, his assistant, a petite blonde bundle of energy, came into his office and interrupted his musings. "It's getting a lot worse outside. I let the office staff go home early to beat the traffic jams that are certain to occur," she announced.

"Fine," said Spence, who was ready to leave anyway. He had promised earlier to meet a group of his friends at Dooley's after work for happy hour. *Wish I had not made that commitment,* he thought.

The short walk from his office to Dooley's reminded him that he would need to retrace his steps to retrieve his car. However, parking around Dooley's was usually marginal at best. Spence hoped that Colleen would be there this evening, but with the snow, she may have gone on home.

Big John greeted him as he came in. "Your party is gathering in the back room," he announced. Four other men who worked in his office were already there, loudly discussing the latest political upheaval in Washington and its effects on the stock market. Two women were also there; one he did not recognise, but the other was Colleen.

Colleen Brannon was thirty years old with two children. She had lost her husband four years ago in an automobile accident that also almost killed her. The children were in the backseat unharmed. Although they had good insurance, the bills were enormous, and she had to start working. She reactivated her realtor's license and was now working for Kelly Williams Realty Elite, a small but very successful firm dealing with high-end properties. She had sold Spence his new home last summer, and at $2.6 million, it was one of her best sales of the year.

Colleen had loved working with Spence on the sale. He was good-looking, extremely mannerly, and had, as she said, "a British accent to die for". Her only problem was that he was black, and she was from an old family from Charleston, South Carolina. Following the sale, Spence had asked her to dinner to celebrate. Her South Carolina heritage gave her considerable reservations about interracial dating. Eventually she agreed and met him for dinner, but they never got beyond that point. They would occasionally meet at Dooley's with a group of people they both knew.

Tonight was no different, except that it was snowing much harder now. Spence moved over to her table and sat down beside her.

"Your kids doing OK?" he inquired. It was always a safe opening.

"Martin has finally finished soccer, but he is now into band," she said.

"Sally started second grade and is doing very well. They are planning on spending the night with my sister and her kids this evening, for which I'm very glad considering how hard it is snowing. How do you like your new house by now?"

"It's not Jamaica, but it is certainly better than living in New York City."

"Spence, I'm sorry I put you off a few months ago when you asked me to go out with you. I am still having a lot of problems getting over the loss of David."

"Don't give it a thought," he said. "I have been busy with my new clients and the drastic market fluctuations. Any plans for tonight?"

"Not really. I've been working on the sale of a condo in the McNulty Tower building. I've had a cleaning crew there all week. It was a mess from the previous owners, who were heavy smokers. We're just about finished, however. They finished cleaning the carpets and drapes today. The walls were painted last week, and all of the furniture was cleaned".

"Rather than go out and fight the snow, we could just have another drink here. The food at Dooley's is better than most of the other local restaurants. Best of all, we don't have to leave," said Spence.

They talked for a while, and finally their friends finished their drinks and left. They were alone. Megan brought out two heaping plates of fish and chips and another Guinness each. "Will there be anything else?" she asked.

"We are fine," answered Spence.

"Spence, I have always wanted to ask you something. Have you ever come close to getting married?"

"Yes. I had a girl in Montego Bay that I would've married in a heartbeat, but she did not want to leave Jamaica, and I did not want to spend the rest of my life there. It was an irreconcilable problem. She finally married my cousin a few years ago, and so the case is closed. Your husband has been gone, what, four years now? No boyfriends or relationships for you?"

"I dated a guy off and on for a while last summer. He worked for Century 21 and was divorced. I eventually found out why he was divorced," she explained. "Aside from him, I've dated a few other men. Generally one date is enough. When they find out that I have two young children, most men lose interest very rapidly. The children and my job keep me plenty busy."

It was close to ten o'clock, and the last of the patrons were venturing out into the still-falling snow. "I really don't want to drive home. The kids are gone for the weekend, so I will probably crash at the condo. Since I've been working in and out of there for the past month, I keep a change of clothes and bathroom essentials there, almost like travelling on the road. It is fully furnished and finally clean," she said as they got up to leave.

"My car is in the Plaza Bank building parking garage, so I will be walking that direction. Let me walk you home," Spence offered.

"That would be very good of you," she replied.

They turned left out of Dooley's and headed onto Fore Street, walking slightly uphill. The snow had slackened, but many inches of new snow were covering the last footprints on the sidewalk. Very little traffic ventured out on the snow-packed streets. They could see red and blue flashing lights a block over.

"Someone just had a bad ending to their evening," Spence observed. "I've been in the United States now for over ten years, and I still don't like to drive in snow."

Spence took her arm and held her close to him to steady her as they walked through the ankle-deep snow. She did not object. In fact, she found the sensation very pleasant. *OK, some things about snow are all right,* she thought.

They reached McNulty Tower, and she used her card key to pass through the lobby entrance door. Spence followed her inside. George, the night security person, looked up from his monitors, acknowledged her, and discreetly returned his gaze to his work.

After a few moments of awkward silence, they both spoke simultaneously. "Thanks for a good evening, I will go retrieve my car and fight the roads home," he said.

"It's not too late. Would you like to come up for a nightcap? I know there is a good bottle of Pinot in the wine bar," she said.

They both laughed, and without hesitation Spence replied, "Maybe one glass will be OK."

They rode up the elevator in silence. Colleen thought, *Even people who know each other seldom talk on an elevator. There must be some unspoken rule about that.*

They got off on the top floor and went down the short hall to the central foyer, where doorways opened into the four condos that occupied the top of the building.

Using her card key, she opened the door for them. She took Spence's coat and hung it on a rack by the door. "Let me show you around." She went into realtor mode. "Eighteen hundred square feet, and a steal at $1.8 million."

"That's almost as much I paid for that huge home you sold me," Spence said incredulously.

"Amazingly enough, someone will buy it. I've already had a couple who want to see it as soon as the clean-up is finished. You may know some of the regulars from Dooley's who live in the apartment section of this building. Only the top two floors have condos. The wine is in the bar refrigerator. Mind pouring two glasses for us? I need to freshen up a bit." She disappeared into the bedroom area.

Spence found the wine, opened the bottle, and poured two glasses. He walked to the large picture window looking down on the ocean side of Portland. The snow was still falling about as hard as it had been all evening. The lights of a freighter were just barely visible offshore. The streets were completely deserted except for an ambulance headed for St Mary's Hospital.

Colleen soon returned. She had changed from her work clothes into a pale blue blouse and white slacks with no shoes. A large leather couch faced the window. She sat down and motioned for Spence to join her. He handed her a glass of wine and sat beside her. They both sipped their wine in silence for a few moments, gazing out at the vista in front of them.

"So $1.8 million?" said Spence.

"Yep, but what a view."

Spence finished his wine and got up, preparing to leave. "I really need to get going home. As you know, it's not too far, but I'll bet that the roads have not been ploughed as yet."

Colleen walked him to the door and retrieved his coat. "Thanks for walking me home. I'm just glad I don't have to drive home tonight."

They held each other's gaze for a few moments at the door. Spence again thanked her for the wine, turned, and headed for the elevator. Colleen watched him walk down the short corridor that guarded the four units on this floor.

I bet he turns around and looks back, she thought. He did.

The next few weeks were very busy for both of them. Spence was occupied with his clients, and Colleen sold the condo to the interested couple. This one sale alone netted her a commission larger than what David would have earned in a year. *Not bad for a few months' effort,* she thought.

Groundhog Day was cold and rainy. Spence had been told that in Pennsylvania, the large rodent saw his shadow, foretelling six more weeks of snow. That was not what he wanted to hear. *But the creature, for all of its legendary prognosticating powers, could be wrong,* he hoped.

Spence had become a Friday night regular at Dooley's—something that he looked forward to, hoping that Colleen would also show up. Colleen remained in the back of his memory, occasionally drifting to the foreground, especially while he was standing in the large windows of his home looking at the windswept Atlantic crashing on the rocks below. The big house was empty and always lonely.

Latasha flew for American Airlines and was now in her fourth year as a flight attendant. Spence had met her last month on a short hop from Portland to Cleveland. She had openly flirted with him in the first-class cabin most of the trip, making it clear that she would be in Portland in a few weeks and would like to have dinner, if he was interested. They had agreed on a date to meet at Dooley's because she knew that location.

Latasha made a grand entrance into Dooley's, and Big John looked up at Spence and winked. "That is one good-looking lady! She could attend to me any time," he said to Spence.

Megan poked him in the ribs. "John, she probably is a very proper lady," she said with a sly glance towards Spence, who was now totally embarrassed by the conversation.

Latasha was gorgeous with light chocolate skin, a beautiful face, short hair, and a phenomenal figure. "Hard to resist that," said John.

She walked up to Spence, shook the water from her scarf and coat, and sat down on the stool next to him. "Told you I would meet you! Bet you thought I would be a no-show."

"You said you would be here, and I always believe the lady," replied Spence. They ordered a Guinness apiece and engaged in small talk.

"Care for another?" asked Megan.

"No, thanks. I think we will go to Michael's for dinner," replied Spence.

Latasha took his arm as they left to walk the two blocks to Michael's. The rain had let up, and it was about as far to his car in the bank building parking garage as it was to Michael's.

"Where do you stay when you fly into Portland?" he inquired.

"The beautiful Holiday Inn Express. I am rooming with another flight attendant," she replied.

Michael's was a very expensive, upscale restaurant overlooking the harbour. The food and wine were excellent. *Latasha eats like this was her last meal,* thought Spence as she finished the last role in the basket.

"They have cherries jubilee on the menu," she said. "Can we try that? It's one of my favourites."

The dessert was flamed perfectly at the table side. They finished with a small glass of ice wine. Latasha had gone from touching casually to now holding his hand across the table.

"I had a fabulous time. I can't remember a better dinner or a better dinner companion," she said softly to Spence. "What do you want to do now?"

Spence knew what he wanted to do, and so did she. They walked hand in hand out of the restaurant. The rain had now stopped. The cityscape reflected in geometric patterns off the wet, deserted, cobblestone street.

"We could go to your place," she offered. "My roommate won't mind if I don't show up. My flight out is not until 3.30 tomorrow afternoon, so we have lots of time to get acquainted."

The warnings were there. *This is moving way too fast,* he thought, but a gorgeous, willing woman and a backlog of testosterone overwhelmed all logic. They found his Range Rover and were soon heading north out of town. Her hand teasing his leg only increased the desire, and all caution was soon thrown to the wind.

They passed through the security gate, waved in by the guard on duty. "Oh, my God. These are gorgeous homes. And you live here?" she asked.

They parked under the portico, and he helped her out of the Range

Rover. Spence opened the front door and ushered her into the entryway, helping her out of her coat and tucking it into the guest coat closet. She walked on into the interior of the house, stopping in the great room with its high vaulted ceiling and windows from floor to the point of the peak.

"Is that the ocean out there?" she asked. "Do you even have a beach?"

"No beach, just a cliff and rocks to the ocean," Spence replied.

She walked around in obvious awe. "I've never been in a home this beautiful. A gorgeous guy, lots of money, a good job, and not married?" She stopped midsentence and blurted out, "Oh, shit—you're gay, aren't you?"

All caution now gone, he reached from behind her and wrapped his arms around her with his hands caressing her breasts. "No, the thought never entered my mind." He pressed up against her bottom from the backside. "Gay I am definitely not."

"Can I see the rest of the house?" she asked.

"How about a glass of wine?" Spence suggested. "Then the full tour."

With a glass of Pinot in hand, they first looked at the huge granite and stainless steel kitchen with windows opening across the dining area to the ocean. "This room is bigger than my entire apartment in Cleveland," she said. "Do you cook?"

"Sometimes I do, if I have the time," he replied.

The formal dining area was similar to the great room, with a vaulted ceiling and floor-to-ceiling glass windows. She rubbed her hands along the back of a soft vanilla-coloured leather couch in front of the window. "This is absolutely amazing," she said.

Spence skilfully bypassed most of the house, ending up in the master bedroom. He showed her the bath with a Jacuzzi tub looking out on the same seascape.

"Let's get in the tub," she suggested, and without waiting for a response, she started taking off her clothes. She soon stood in front of a startled Spence totally naked. Her figure was gorgeous as he had anticipated. Spence could not take his eyes off of her solidly built, perfect body.

He turned the water on in the tub using a remote, gathered up her clothes, and took them into the bedroom. He re-entered the bathroom now devoid of clothing to find her sitting on the edge of the tub, her feet in the swirling pool.

He sat down beside her, and they slipped down into the hot, foaming water. Her lips locked onto his, and they kissed deeply, her free hand now firmly grasping his erect organ. His hands roved over her perfect body. With no further encouragement needed, she straddled his lap and pushed him deep into her.

The dramatic change was instantaneous from a soft, passionate woman, to a wild beast thrashing hard and fast against him as she immediately entered her first orgasm. Her fingernails dug into the skin of his back, and she clawed all the way down to his waist with such force that she drew eight long, bloody gashes from shoulder to waist.

The dark eyes that only moments before had been so seductive were now wide and burning into his soul. She threw her head back and screamed as she vaulted into another violent orgasm, her eyes wild and her mouth wide open. She continued to scream and thrash through one orgasm after another, her nails now dug firmly into both of his arms, penetrating the skin. Blood stained the water in the Jacuzzi as she clamped her open mouth against the skin of his lower neck and bit deeply until she drew blood. The water was now a foaming red froth. She continued to alternately bite and scream, pressing wildly against his body, each orgasm more violent than the last.

Spence's entire thought process at this moment was how to escape from this insane creature he had invited into his home. He managed to rip himself free of her and violently pushed her back against the other side of the Jacuzzi, his blood dripping from her mouth, a red froth on the water's surface. He seriously contemplated drowning her but thought better of it.

She gathered her legs under her, screamed, and lunged at him again, hands outstretched and mouth open. She was unbelievably strong, but before she could grab hold of him again, he slapped her violently against the side of her face, knocking her back against the edge of the tub.

"Stop, you crazy bitch! What's wrong with you?"

This only increased her resolve as she felt the side of her face still stinging where he had slapped her. "Do it again!" she said as she lunged at him again, mouth wide open and eyes flashing fire.

This time Spence did not hold back, striking her on the side of her head with the heel of his hand hard enough to daze her and make her stop for a moment.

He dragged her out of the Jacuzzi and onto the carpeted floor of the bathroom, held her face down, and wrapped her arms to her side with a large bath towel. He turned her face up, tightening the towel around her.

"What in the hell happened? What came over you?" he asked incredulously.

Latasha now much calmer. She looked at him, tears streaming down her face and Spence's blood still dripping from the corner of her mouth. Spence turned off the Jacuzzi pump, and the red froth began to subside.

She was still breathing heavily but no longer crying or screaming. Spence again asked, "What in God's name happened to you?"

"I don't know. I am so sorry. I sometimes lose myself when I have sex. My doctor says that I have something called bipolar syndrome. I'm OK now." She smiled at him. "Want to try it again, but slower?"

"Woman, you may call it bipolar, but I sure as hell don't want a rerun. One of us won't survive another engagement like that."

"Spence, I am so sorry. It won't happen again," she pleaded.

"It sure as shit won't happen again," said Spence as he cautiously let her up off the floor and retrieved her clothing. "Get dressed. I'm taking you back to the Holiday Inn. I never want to see or hear from you again. You are in serious need of good medical help, and I'm going to have to go by the emergency room and get stitches and a tetanus shot."

When John asked him a few days afterwards how his date had gone, he sidestepped the question quickly. "She was a little bit different and definitely not my type." It took Spence many months to put memories of the night of Latasha behind him.

Spring had finally subdued winter. Leaves were appearing on the trees, and the first week of June banished the thoughts of the winter snow and ice, at least for a few months. Spence was taking a lunch break on a park bench just outside of his office building when a familiar voice interrupted him.

"Good morning, stranger. Haven't seen you for a long time." Spence turned to see Colleen standing beside him. "How is everything going?"

Spence replied, "It has been a long, slow winter. I'm glad warm weather is finally here. I did get adventurous a few weeks ago and bought a small sailboat, which I'm planning to take out for the first time this weekend."

"I love sailboats," replied Colleen.

Our family always had a sailboat, and my father taught me to sail when

I was very young. It has been years since I've had my feet on a deck. Want some help? I'm a pretty good mate."

"That would be fantastic," replied Spence. "The boat is a catamaran and easy enough for one person to handle, but it's always much simpler if there are two people who know what they're doing. When I was a youngster in Jamaica, we always had access to one or more sailboats. The waters along the north coast of Jamaica are fantastic sailing waters, and of course there was always the rum trade." He laughed. "Seriously though, I've been on boats since I could walk. A boat was not practical in New York City, but here a lot of people have them, and Portland has a nice marina."

"What kind of a boat did you get?" she asked.

"A three-year-old Tomcat catamaran 970S, thirty-two-foot single mast," he replied.

"If you are serious, I can hardly wait. Saturday morning?" she offered.

"This will be my first time out on open water in the boat. I sailed it around the bay a few times with the dealer that I bought it from, but this'll be the first time out in the Atlantic. Saturday morning at eight, at Ed's Marina."

"I will be there," she agreed.

The following Saturday morning, Spence looked up from the boat's cabin. Colleen stood in the doorway wearing a see-through cover-up. Her swimsuit set off a very nice figure. Her dark hair, normally worn in a tight style, now flowed around her shoulders. "I brought a jacket because it usually gets cool on the water," she said. "I also packed a lunch in case we decide to stay out longer."

"That is fantastic. There's already beer and soft drinks in the cooler," Spence replied as he helped her down into the spacious cabin area. "I love catamarans because there's much more room for both deck and living space on them."

Colleen made herself at home as if she had done this all her life. She quickly identified cabinet space for the items that she brought on board. "The refrigerator is not turned on, and I have a few things that need cooling. Do you want them in the ice chest, or do you want me to turn the refrigerator on?"

"If you know how to start it, that's fine. The dealer didn't show me how that worked."

Soon everything was stowed, and they went topside. Colleen stepped onto the dock, pulled the shore power plug, cast off the tie-downs, and stepped back on the deck. "Ready to go, Captain," she stated in her most nautical voice.

Spence started the two outboard engines and deftly manoeuvred out of the slip and into the narrow waterway of the marina. As soon as they had cleared the marina, he and Colleen raised the mainsail. He cut the engines, and they were moving on wind power alone, heading towards the breakwater of the harbour. Once clear of the harbour, Colleen raised the jib, and they picked up a good wind and moved swiftly along the shoreline, aiming for a small group of islands a few miles north-east of Portland across Luckse Sound. The boat handled perfectly, and both of them had more fun than they'd had in a long time.

After about an hour of sailing, a small chain of barrier islands appeared before them. They approached one of the larger islands and dropped anchor just off the island in the lee of the wind. Colleen fixed a snack and two beers. The early summer sunshine was warm, and there was almost no breeze. Spence was stripped down to his bathing trunks, and Colleen was in her swimsuit. Both of them stretched out on the trampoline area between the hulls.

Spence lay on his stomach. Without thinking, Colleen reached over and rubbed the skin across his well-muscled back, noting the symmetrical lines of still healing scars running the full length of his torso. "How did you get these?" she inquired.

"It's a long but actually a very short story," Spence replied. "Let's just say it was the result of a very bad decision on my part."

"She must've been pretty aggressive," Colleen retorted.

"Aggressive is a relatively mild term for the encounter. This was a lesson well learned," replied Spence as he rolled over on his back and propped up on one elbow, taking in all of Colleen's features. "Anyone in your life yet?"

"Nope, only my Century 21 experience, which does not sound quite as bad as yours. He keeps trying, but he is simply not my type. My sister has the kids today—opening day at the animal park—so you and I are it."

Spence reached over and held her hand. "I would like it to be more than just one day," he said.

She squeezed his hand back and leaned over, and for the first time their lips met in a very light kiss.

They were suddenly interrupted by rapid shift in the wind as a gust swung the boat around on its anchor.

"So much for a nice summer day," Spence said as he studied a low bank of clouds forming up from the south. "We'd better get moving before we get wet."

Spence hauled the anchor, and Colleen raised the sails. The wind quickly caught the sheets and they were soon heading back to the harbour, but the squall line beat them. Colleen pulled in the jib. By now the rain was coming down in torrents. Spence finally had to drop the sail and use the engines to keep them on a straight course back to Portland. They passed the outer harbour light when the rain stopped, and Spence took them in to the dock under engine power. He was still compensating for a strong crosswind, but he smoothly guided the boat into the slip. Colleen jumped off and quickly secured the tie-downs. Spence wrapped the sails and closed all the remaining hatches. He flipped on the automatic bilge pump, connected shore power, and stepped out onto the dock.

"Ship is secure, mate," he announced. "That was a fantastic sail, rain and all. You did all that as well as anyone I have ever sailed with."

"It all comes back when needed," she replied.

They walked hand in hand up the ramp to the parking lot. "Next Saturday?" inquired Spence.

"Absolutely, but we may have to take two passengers," she said.

"No problem. I would love to meet your kids. I've heard so much about them from you."

The following weekend turned out to be cold and rainy, with the forecast to continue through the first part of the following week. Colleen extended her babysitter for Friday evening, and they met at Dooley's. They shared their sailing adventures with James and Suzanne Rowe. James was one of Spence's investment clients. The Rowes were quite excited and of course wanted to be invited on the next cruise.

"I have never been on a sailboat," said James. "What is required?"

"Nothing but a bathing suit, deck shoes, and sunscreen," replied Spence.

Suzanne sized up Spence. *He would sure be a lot of fun without the bathing suit. I'm not sure that Colleen would go along with it, though.*

The following weekend turned out to be perfect. The storm front had finally cleared the area, and a cool north-east breeze foretold a perfect sailing weekend. Colleen and her children—Martin, ten years old, and Sally, who was eight—had never been on a boat before.

By nine o'clock they had all of the supplies on board. Colleen cast off the shorelines, and they were underway out of the harbour. Once clear of the other boats, Spence gave both children specific tasks to do to help sail the boat. Spence had two younger siblings, but he had never been very much involved with children before. They fully accepted him as "Mother's friend" and never gave the colour difference any thought at all; he was Mr Thomas, and that was it.

Spence found one of the small offshore islands and anchored the boat, and all of them played for many hours in the relatively shallow, warm water and on the sandy beach. Colleen had prepared a sumptuous lunch, and the day went much too rapidly for all of them.

Two weeks passed before they were able to get back out on the boat again. Colleen's sister had the children for the weekend, and Spence and Colleen planned a much longer trip that would keep them out overnight as they worked their way north-east along the string of small islands and peninsulas that flanked the Maine coastline.

By late afternoon, Spence had selected a small, secluded bay along the deserted coastline south of the Marshall Point lighthouse, and he dropped anchor. Colleen fixed an excellent dinner of cheese, fruit, and cold salmon. They enjoyed a glass of a late harvest wine and watched the sunset.

"Spence, you and I have known each other now for almost a full year, and we've never gotten much further than handholding and a light kiss. I know that I was hesitant at first, but now I have no reservations at all." She leaned across the small table separating the deck chairs and gave him a long, deep kiss.

They leaned back and looked into each other's eyes. "Are you sure you're ready for this?" asked Spence.

In response, Colleen slipped out of her bikini top and stood up. There was no chance of her missing the significant bulge that formed in Spence's bathing suit. She took his hand and led him into the master stateroom. She turned to face him and dropped the bottom of her bathing suit.

Spence was beyond restraint and released himself from the confines of his garments. They stood for a moment, taking in all of the features of each other's bodies. Then a slow kiss escalated into tentative exploration of each other.

Colleen lay down on the soft bed, and Spence lay beside her, continuing his explorations until Colleen could no longer resist. She straddled him, taking his erection to full depth. She moved ever so slowly and then with more vigour until she reached the most satisfying orgasm that she could recall.

Spence was patient and an excellent lover. They tried classic positions and a few unconventional moves until both of them were completely spent. They lay in each other's arms, lolled to sleep with the gentle rocking of the boat and the sheer exhaustion and satisfaction of the evening.

Spence had patiently waited for her to finally decide when and where, and he had always been comfortable with this arrangement. Their lovemaking was both gentle and passionate, and it released many long years and memories and relegated them to past experiences, with tonight being the only time and place of any importance for the two of them. As pleasant experiences often did, the weekend moved much too fast, but it was perfect.

Her children were delighted when she announced to them that she and Spence were to be married.

Conclusion

This chapter covers two issues that can beset couples more frequently than we suspect. The controversial, and often difficult to reconcile and overcome, issue of the prejudice of black on white. Neither Spence nor Colleen was comfortable with the concept at first. It was only after other unsuccessful attempts at same-colour unions that they found colour really plays no role at all. In the end, it is the person and how you are attracted that truly matters. Your heart can eventually overrule ingrained ideas of what is right or proper or acceptable. Spence and Colleen were fortunate;

fifty years ago, this would have been very difficult, and one hundred years ago it would have been almost impossible and even illegal in some places.

Violence often accompanies sexual activity. It is usually instigated by the male, but a dominant female can be just as aggressive. Some people need the violence to achieve sexual satisfaction; some are able to achieve orgasm without any intimate sexual contact, getting off from the violence. Whether these people are truly bipolar or have even deeper problems is a medical issue that is often extremely difficult to diagnose and overcome. Persons with violent personalities may appear normal, but they almost always give clues early on. The other party frequently ignores these clues, common sense being overridden by the moment. Many times these encounters can go on for years, the dominant member convincing the subordinate partner that he or she deserves the punishment and violence.

Questions

1) What could Spence have done to prevent the uncomfortable episode with Latasha?
2) Do you accept biracial alliances as part of ordinary life? If you met a person of another race who seemed attractive, would you consider having a relationship with him or her?
3) Spence was from a wealthy Jamaican family. Would the likelihood of your accepting a person of a different race be changed by his or her country or the circumstances of origin?
4) Spence and Colleen shared several factors in common. How did their professional lives, origins, families, and hobbies influence their relationship?
5) The sailboat finally became the common factor that allowed them to form a bond. Do you think they could have done this as easily, or even at all, without some common uniting factor?
6) Were you surprised that it took them so long to become intimate?

CHAPTER 13

KK

Karl Kilgore Henderson, MD, hated his name. From a very early age, he was always known simply as KK. KK was now thirty-seven years old and a professor of clinical psychiatry at the university medical school. He was divorced, his ex-wife had custody of their 2 children, and he did not do much outside of work. He always wore dark, horn-rimmed Prada glasses that accented the small, natty black moustache and his jet-black hair. He always dressed as though he was going to a business meeting.

KK was a regular at Dooley's. He was unbelievably good at picking up lonely businesswomen at the bar. He always told Big John it was for their own good, not necessarily just for sex—although that was also usually very good if it occurred. John was never fully convinced that KK wasn't just a sexual predator.

Megan told John, "These women sometimes return months later on a subsequent trip to town, and they always ask about KK. I have even been asked if I could locate KK for them. Maybe he really does provide some therapeutic benefit." She laughed.

Big John continued to remain suspicious and sceptical.

Tuesday evening was usually quiet at Dooley's. KK sat at the bar, working on his first gin and tonic. She made eye contact with him as soon as she walked through the door. She headed directly to where KK was sitting and selected the stool next to him, even though the bar was less than half full of patrons.

A few moments of silence followed her ordering a gin and tonic. She finally looked at KK. "You here on business too?"

"No, I actually live here. I just like to stop by Dooley's and unwind occasionally," he replied very casually.

KK had an uncanny way of allowing women to immediately warm up him without ever making the first overt move. He'd once told Big John, "I have never made the first advance towards a woman. They always ask me first." Tonight was no exception.

"My name is Sally Hammond, and you?"

"Just call me KK. I don't really like my full name," KK replied.

"That is very mysterious," Sally retorted.

"OK, it's Karl Kilgore Henderson. Now you see why I like to be called KK."

"That sort of makes sense. I still like the name Karl, but KK it is. So you live here in Portland? What sort of work do you do?" she inquired.

"I am a clinical psychiatrist at the university teaching hospital. I specialise in sexual dysfunction therapy. Admittedly, it is a rather odd and highly specialised field."

"No kidding? That sounds like a fascinating field," she replied.

KK skilfully left her introductory statements hanging and then asked, "What brings you to Portland?"

"I'm the business manager for a large medical practice in Hartford, Connecticut. I'm here attending a course on compliance and Medicare regulations. Rather boring, but very necessary in today's world," she replied.

"So you are also in a medically related occupation?"

"I guess so." She returned to KK's specialty. "What does a doctor whose expertise is in sexual dysfunction actually do?"

"It's a very complex field, mostly consisting of talking through the problems that couples experience after they are married. Sexual dysfunction often occurs later in the marriage, after the children are grown," KK answered.

"Why does that happen?" Sally inquired.

"Life and sex become routine. Routine is usually followed by boredom, and the couple shuts down sexually or goes off to find satisfaction elsewhere. Surprisingly, it is often the woman who strays first," explained KK.

"That is all very intriguing. Because neither of us seems to have anything better to do right now, would you open to answering a few questions that have been puzzling me?"

That's how it always works, thought KK. *She just warmed up to the subject faster than most women.* "Sure," he replied. "Just be aware that questions often lead to more questions. We could spend a lot of time talking about the subject."

"I certainly don't have any plans for the evening, or I would not be sitting at a bar talking to a stranger about sexual habits." She laughed.

"All right. Let's go to one of the back tables, where we will have a little more privacy. I am open to you asking me anything that comes to mind. If you don't object, in order for me to better understand what you want to know, I may ask you some rather blunt questions in return."

"That's totally fine by me. I have a few questions I always wanted to have an opportunity to ask someone who just might have an answer," she replied.

They selected one of the back tables at Dooley's, and Megan brought their drinks to the table. "First, you have to hear a short lecture to set the theme of our discussion," KK explained. He launched into his teaching mode, and Sally hung on to his every word. "A strong and unfettered sex life plays a very important role in true love. Sexual interaction is ageless, from adolescent exploration to the old couple holding hands in the grocery store. Sexual activity can be random, selected, chaotic, forced, violent, consensual, unfettered, constrained, and a multitude of other descriptive adjectives. A marriage, and even a person's life, stagnates when sexual interaction ceases."

Sally replied, "That certainly fits me. I'm forty-two years old and have been married since I was nineteen to the same man. I have three children, and the last of them is still in college; the other two are married and gone. George and I get along great, and we don't fight or argue over much of anything, but we don't interact anymore. We always had ceremonial sex on our wedding anniversary; he even forgot that last year."

"Do you still have sex with him at all?" KK asked.

"Usually if I initiate it, we have reasonably good sex. We always enjoyed sex in the past, but it seems to be too much trouble to get started," she ruefully said.

"Do you think George is straying on the outside?"

"I don't know. How would you actually know that?" Sally questioned.

"There are usually subtle signs; we can go over some of those later. Have you ever considered straying outside of your marital constraints?"

"Actually, in all honesty, I have fantasised about having sex with the husband of a couple whom we see socially. I know that he is attracted to me, and I am very much attracted to him, but we have never taken it beyond casual touching when we are together. At a New Year's Eve party last year, we had our first kiss, and I would've taken him to bed right then if it had been possible. His wife is a very good friend of mine, and we frequently discuss our mutual slowdown of sexual activity across a cup of coffee. As you said, we seem to have stagnated," Sally answered.

"So the basic answer is no, but under the right circumstances, you probably would?" inquired KK.

"Yes, I probably would, given the right opportunity. Is this wrong? Is this sinful? Is this morally reprehensible?"

"There is no correct answer to that question. Sexual freedom and marital infidelity is as old as history. Only the individual can pass judgement upon his or her own moral or ethical constraints. Given the opportunity, George is probably even more likely to stray than you are. Having sex with a good friend is much more likely to lead to long-term marital complications than having sex with someone outside of your circle of close friends and acquaintances."

"Do you all do anything creative sexually, or is it just standard, missionary-style sex?" KK inquired.

"Neither of us was experienced. I'm sure we were both probably virgins—certainly I was—when we got married, and so we never ventured outside of conventional positions. Sex education is woefully inadequate, usually relying upon bad information from your peers and little or no information from your parents. I have read some sex manuals, but they are all very graphic and at the same time not specific enough to understand well. They make it look so complicated and, frankly, embarrassing," Sally explained.

"That begins to explain some of the basic problems that you are experiencing. This is not uncommon at all. When a couple's entire sexual experience consists of only the basic act of copulation, then a very critical piece of complete and fulfilling love begins to fade with the female menopause and will totally disappear with the male menopause. The marriage may fail or become meaningless unless the remaining bonds of love are very strong," KK explained. "Was your sex life ever very good, even in the beginning?"

"When we were just married, we had sex every night for a long time. I vividly remember the first time that we did not have sex. I guess George had a very bad day at work, and he said he was tired and went to sleep. I must've cried half of the night, wondering what I had done wrong. It was only later when I too needed a night off that I realised that you cannot go on at that rate forever. Once a day stretched out to once a week, and then less frequently. Children certainly get in the way and are a good excuse. Now, I can hardly remember the last time that we actually did have sex. God, I just can't believe that I'm telling you all of this."

"Don't worry. I have heard all of this more times than I can count," KK explained. "Are you sure that George is not having sex outside of your marriage that you don't know about?"

"I really don't think so, but I guess there's no good way to know. My friends are always eager to tell me about someone who is sleeping around, but so far if they know anything about George, they've not mentioned it—yet."

"People are usually reasonably clever about covering up affairs, but then they become casual and get sloppy, someone finds out, and there's always the well-meaning friend who says, *You really need to know this,*" KK said. "Short relationships are seldom a problem; they usually result from the same circumstances you are describing. They are soon over and done with. A long-term affair is generally much more complicated, and ultimately the couple has to decide what they're going to do about it. The only two options are to live with it or to divorce. Here's a very important question. Do you really like sex? Are you satisfied with it? If not, what could you do to enhance the relationship? Have you ever thought about what you could do to add more interest to your sex life? What could you and George do to improve the experience?"

"Of course I think about it a lot," Sally replied. "I do like sex, however I think there should be more to it than I am experiencing. The sex manuals indicate a much more complicated bunch of positions, but they really don't go into any detail about partner satisfaction. I am sure that everybody thinks or worries about what they could do to better satisfy their partners, and in doing so perhaps better satisfy themselves. George just finishes and seems to be content, but often I would like to continue. Is this not a common problem? My real question is where does one find truly authoritative, as well as clearly understandable, information?"

"Very perceptive," answered KK. "There are a lot of ways that you can gain the type of information, and even experience, that you are seeking. If you can become better educated on the talents and techniques of sexual interplay, then both you and your partner will achieve a much higher level of satisfaction. The question is where you can find the type of information that you are seeking. Most sex manuals are woefully inadequate, as you have described. Sex education courses and psychiatric help are two acceptable sources. Your best source of information, in all honesty, is my website. I offer specific lessons in the various types of sexual dysfunction and an ongoing monthly newsletter related to sexual problems in general. I can give you a link to that website, which both you and George need to share. The two of you should find this information very interesting and extremely helpful.

"Perhaps an unacceptable answer, but by far the best educational course, is firsthand experience with someone who understands the needs of both the male and the female partner."

"And who just might be that person?" Asked Sally with a sly grin as she placed her hand on KK's arm.

KK feigned a look of shock and embarrassment, but he could not maintain his composure. "If you feel adventurous this evening, we might see if there are some lessons to be learned."

Sally replied without hesitation. "I certainly think an evening educational course would be well appreciated." She drifted her hand along his arm and across the back of his hand.

KK paid the bar tab, and they walked out the door arm in arm.

John looked at Megan. "See? He did it again."

"John," said Megan, "I was paying more attention than you were; it was very apparent to me that she made the first move from the time she walked through the door until she eventually picked him up. It is amazing how he does that. The guy is good!"

"Honestly, I think he is no more than a male hooker. He comes to a bar, picks up a woman, and promptly takes her to bed." John explained.

"I know for some underlying reason you really don't like KK, but really he's no different than most of the guys who come in there looking for a pickup and a good time. He is just consistent," Megan replied.

"All women seem to like KK," John grumbled. "But I don't have to."

The following week, Mildred was seated at the bar talking to John, and the subject of KK and his predatory approach to women came up. "Megan seems to think that the women pick him up, but I am sure that he is using his charm to prey upon their vulnerability. I personally think he's nothing more than a male hooker!" John emphatically stated.

Mildred replied, "KK is one of those people whom I have known for many years, but I never considered him one of my close friends. He and I do talk occasionally, but I really don't know that much about him. So you say that he consistently leaves here with a good-looking woman?"

"Well, not every time, but I would say three out of four times, he leaves here with a woman. But not all of them are good looking," John answered.

"What do you mean they're not all good-looking?" inquired Mildred.

"He never seems to attract younger women. The ones that he is attracted to are almost always in their thirties or forties, or perhaps even older, and not every one of them is what I would consider a good looker," John answered.

"John, don't you find that a little unusual? Most guys go for the young, good-looking girls in a bar. Somebody as suave and dapper as KK should always be able to attract young, good-looking girls. Maybe he really is offering marriage and sexual counselling?"

"I just think he feeds them a very good line of BS, or maybe he is hypnotising them," John theorised.

He might be an interesting challenge I had never considered, Mildred thought.

As she was mulling this concept over, KK strolled into the bar and took a seat next to her. "Slow evening Mildred?"

"I might ask you the same question, KK. You are seldom in here without a female companion," she retorted.

"I have no idea what you're talking about," he replied.

"Oh, bullshit. Of course you do. It is common knowledge that you are seldom without a different, good-looking woman any given night of the week. You are a natural charmer, and you know it."

"OK, sure. Not much happening right now. I don't come in here looking for a pickup—they just seem to find me. Mildred, we have known each other for many years. You know I have a special talent with women. I can't help it. I love women, and for some reason they love and trust me," KK answered. "You should understand this, Mildred—you also have multiple male acquaintances."

"Believe me, I know perfectly well what you're talking about. You have tried your charms on me a few times in the past."

"Mildred, answer me truthfully. Am I different from other men? Women are simply attracted to me. Mostly middle-aged businesswomen, not necessarily looking for companionship or a good time; they just zero in on me. At the slightest mention of my specialty of sexual dysfunction, these women instantly bare their souls to me in total confession. It is almost as though I can project the desire for sex into a woman without even talking about it."

"Projected sexual desire seems to be a bit far-fetched," Mildred said.

"That's what I thought too. Many people, both men and women, fantasise about having sex with an acquaintance, or even a stranger sitting next to them. Whether we carry this fantasy all the way through a full sexual encounter or just an interesting survey of the individual is more dependent upon time, place, and person. It's a game I often play to while away the boring time spent attending a long-winded conference, sitting on an airplane, or casually observing a woman at some public gathering. I spend a lot of time flying, which usually presents a myriad of subjects to observe. It doesn't matter whether it's my seatmate, the woman across the aisle, or even the flight attendant; I can conjure up a very interesting fantasy while drifting along in an airplane-induced twilight zone.

"Just as an example, let me tell you what happened to me on a business trip a few months ago. See if you can believe this really occurred.

"I was in the window seat, back row of first class, on an early Friday morning, long non-stop from Los Angeles to Philadelphia. We had no sooner buckled up then she made direct eye contact."

"'I will sure be glad to get back home. This has been a long and difficult week," she initiated. "Since it is the end of the week, I assume you also are going home?'"

"I told her, 'Yes, change planes in Philadelphia. Should be in Portland, Maine, by eight o'clock this evening, if all goes well.'

"We were then interrupted by the usual litany of, *Fasten your seatbelts. The oxygen mask will drop out of a compartment above you. The bag will not inflate. The exit doors are located here and there. Always follow the white lights in the aisle to find the red lights, which indicate the nearest exit after the airplane crashes and is filled with smoke.*

Mildred chuckled at his parody of the all-too-familiar flight attendant announcements.

"My seatmate was a very attractive businesswoman in her early forties; I remember her name was Patricia. With all the noise and confusion of takeoff, we retreated back into the sanctity of our seats until we levelled off and the flight attendant came by to offer the first round of morning libation. Our first bloody mary in hand, Patricia struck up a conversation with me, ultimately leading to the standard question of what do I do. I was straightforward with her and explained I was a psychiatrist specialising in sexual dysfunction. I told her that I had been speaking at a seminar in Los Angeles on this subject. This immediately got her attention, but before she could ask any more questions, the flight attendant brought us breakfast. We had the usual general discussion about why they always have the same omelette on this flight, and then we moved to what a sexual dysfunction therapist does.

"Following breakfast, the flight attendant requested that we close the window shades to darken the cabin, and a dull airplane movie started. Patricia had a third bloody mary, and the conversation became much more specific as she related some of her problems with her travelling and overworked husband. She was very receptive to my discussion on sex therapy and asked a lot of questions."

KK went on to further explain, "I tend to get into a lecture mode and realised that Patricia had drifted off to sleep, her hand still holding my arm, left over from the last intimate question she had asked."

"Breakfast, three drinks, purposeful low oxygen saturation on airplanes, and a darkened cabin, combined with the steady white noise, is very sleep-inducing. I soon drifted into a twilight, not really asleep but not awake, and began to fantasise about making love to my seatmate. I started with gentle kissing. She slowly undressed and stretched out on white satin sheets. She allowed me to advance down to her ample bosom and then on to her belly. After tantalising her for quite some time, I moved on to her wet and willing pelvis," KK explained in a very clinical but sensual tone.

In spite of herself, Mildred could feel that she was getting into the story and was becoming aroused. "Go on, KK. What happened next?"

"Then it really got pretty exciting, because I am certain that she had an orgasm. She screamed and gripped my arm tightly. Of course I immediately woke up, as did she. She was in the aisle seat, and the flight attendant was immediately at her side, very concerned and asking what had happened. Patricia was visibly shaken, breathing heavily, and extremely embarrassed. I immediately interjected that I thought she had just had a very bad dream. She said that she recently had a bad experience flying. The stewardess was still concerned and asked if she could bring her anything. Patricia thanked her and asked for a cup of coffee.

"Patricia knew that I knew what had happened—that she had had an orgasm in her sleep. She proceeded to spend the remainder of the flight asking me how that was possible. She even described in intimate detail the dream that had preceded the orgasm, which was precisely the fantasy that I was projecting. I certainly didn't tell her that I thought I was responsible for it. This was the first time that I had experienced such an event, and I really had no frame of reference. I referred her to my website. She went home to Philadelphia, and I continued on to Portland," KK concluded.

"That was bizarre," said Mildred. "I know you're good, but I really don't think anybody is that good. You had just given her a lot of suggestions, and she had a dream related to your conversation. Or maybe it was some form of hypnosis."

"Mildred, if you are interested and agreeable, I would like to get the perspective of an absolutely unbiased expert in this matter. I want to know if this is even possible," KK said.

"You're telling me that you would like for me to willingly go to sleep beside you, and you will seduce me mentally?" she queried.

"That's exactly what I propose. As I see it, it's the only way that I can prove or disprove that it actually is possible. You and I will both know going into the experiment what we are looking for. You are certainly objective enough to give me a solid analysis and opinion," KK explained

"All right, you definitely have my curiosity aroused. I doubt seriously that you can do this, but let's see. Absolutely no hypnosis, however!" Mildred explained emphatically. "We can go to the cigar room, where it is quiet with more comfortable chairs. There is no one whom I can see in there this evening."

John, in response to the smoke-free environment rules, had made the main bar smoke-free. He then created a small, glass-enclosed, well-appointed room with plush leather chairs and a big-screen TV just for the smokers. He called it the cigar room. He served only premium drinks and offered free hors d'oeuvres from 5 to 7 p.m. each day. A special electrostatic air filtration system kept the room comfortable but still retained the essence of fine tobacco.

Mildred selected the couch and indicated to KK to sit beside her. "Suppose I am your next victim," she said.

"Please, Mildred. I prefer the term new friend. They are never victimised. I never do anything that the woman does not want done to her. I allow her to initiate the first conversation and pose the questions. I only answer, and if requested, I will demonstrate technique," KK replied.

"All right, then. Newfound friend. Step one: I am attracted to you. Now what?" Mildred asked.

"Early on, the conversation comes around to what do I do. I mentioned that I am a clinical psychiatrist and sex therapist specialising in sexual dysfunction. That always piques their interest. If after the introductory pleasantries, a woman initiates the first move at any public meeting, at a bar, a party, or even on an airplane, she has some agenda other than she is just bored. We then become engaged in conversation, and it goes on from there."

"So I have some form of sexual dysfunction that I want to discuss with you? How do I or any other woman get into this conversation?"

"I wait for the opening confession of some disruption in her marital or sexual life. It is always there, and the woman always wants to talk about it. If this does not happen, then the lesson probably also will not happen. I never initiate this discussion; I always wait for the woman to bring up the topic," replied KK.

"What do you mean by lesson?" asked Mildred.

"Sex therapy takes many forms," KK continued. "I can lecture for hours to my classes about the needs and sensitivities of the partners. We can discuss techniques of foreplay, techniques of the various sex acts, and what to do afterwards. All of this is covered in multiple lectures that I give to students. In a condensed form, this is also available in a four-hour series that can be downloaded from my website, along with a monthly newsletter. Obviously someone that I casually meet gets only selected components of this lecture that are specifically directed to the problems and questions that she has broached. I generally end up giving her a free password into my website series. She can introduce the website to her husband, and together this can be very beneficial for them as a couple."

"Do you ever get into this conversation with men?" asked Mildred.

"Very rarely do men ever open up related to any matters of sexual dysfunction. The majority of men are very private about their sexual abilities or inabilities. They frequently take the easy route and blame their wives for any problems they may be experiencing. Generally the mention of sexual dysfunction therapy is enough to send the man back to his laptop, and that's the last I hear from him for the rest of the flight. Women are a totally different story: they really want to discuss their problems.

"Sex therapy is also hands-on, so to speak. One-on-one teaching. I often give private lessons to couples on techniques and learning what needs to be done to bring a partner to truly enjoy sex as a pleasure and not just a duty. Both men and women need coaching and critique on techniques. If a couple is open to learning, I can always add that important piece that was missing. One of the most common complaints that I hear from a couple is that they are out of sync with their partner. They are either ahead or behind; either way, it is a problem of timing. The fault is very often the male, who usually wants to be in control of the relationship."

"You actually teach sex technique?" asked an incredulous Mildred. She thought of her own teaching sessions in the past.

KK said, "Yes, I do, but only to carefully selected individuals or couples. It is a very sensitive and highly personal type of instruction. I keep it very professional and charge a premium hourly rate for my services. These individuals obviously get free access to my website, which is constantly being updated."

"Do you think that there is anything that you could do or advice that you could offer that could possibly improve my sex life or sex technique?" asked a defiant Mildred.

"Mildred, you obviously are a much different situation. You are a long-term acquaintance of mine and are well aware that I have a way with women. You are obviously defensive, not receptive. I would reject you as any type of a client in real life," said KK with a laugh. "However, because you are very perceptive and well aware of me as an individual, I would like to get your absolute objective opinion as to whether I really can subliminally induce sexual thoughts into your mental stream while you are in a twilight sleep. Are you still willing to try this experiment?"

Mildred pondered the proposition for a moment. "OK, no hypnosis. If it works for you, I would like to see if I could do the same thing to you. This would certainly prove your theory—if it works," she said.

"That's an interesting thought," said KK. "No hypnosis, I promise. You will probably go to sleep just out of sheer boredom listening to me talk. I would like to get you to a dreamy or twilight relaxed state, and then I'll see if I can transfer thought to you without actually speaking. The evening is still young. We need another drink to set the mood. This room is absolutely perfect: comfortable chairs, dim lighting, and the ambient white noise background sounds of the ventilation system."

KK motioned through the windows to Megan, who had been obliquely watching them. She responded, and KK ordered another gin and tonic and Mildred had another Guinness. Megan delivered the drinks with a fresh plate of hors d'oeuvres.

"Megan," said KK, "Mildred and I are going to conduct a little clinical experiment and would prefer not to be disturbed for a while."

"No problem," replied an interested Megan. "I will put the private party sign on the door. It's a quiet night, so I'm sure nobody will want the room, and you will not be disturbed. If you need anything, just call."

Megan went back to the bar and told John what she thought was taking place in the cigar room. John just shook his head.

KK and Mildred sat for quite some time, finishing their drinks and chatting about various subjects but always returning to their favourite topic of sexual satisfaction. KK was soon dominating the conversation and had drifted into his monotone lecture mode relating to various sexual techniques. Mildred realised that she was getting drowsy, but she allowed herself to drift off into a twilight zone. As agreed, she was holding KK's hand as he continued his monologue for a few minutes. Then she appeared to be comfortably asleep. KK relaxed, closed his eyes, and began to fantasise about the willing seduction of his companion.

KK first started with gentle kissing and caressing. He visualised her willingly taking off her top. They stretched out comfortably on a large bed, and he continued to advance down to her breasts. He methodically, carefully, and slowly moved across her belly and down to her abdomen. He was gently kissing and caressing, feeling her warmth increase. Even though no physical contact was occurring, he could sense his own arousal as he continued to advance to her warm and willing pelvis. He visualised her pushing his face farther down until he took in her femininity completely.

From the depth of her sleep, Mildred could feel the orgasm coming on and could not hold back. She screamed out in delight, squeezing KK's hand and awakening both of them with a start.

Megan and John looked up from the bar. John shook his head and went back to polishing bar glasses. Megan was far more interested in what had actually happened and made a mental note. *Absolutely have to talk to Mildred about this the next time we meet.*

KK looked at an astonished Mildred, who was still breathing heavily. "Did you actually feel that? Did you have an orgasm?"

"KK, I would never have believed it, but it did actually happen. I was dreaming that someone—I don't think it was you—was making love to me. And yes, I did have not one but a number of orgasms, obviously waking both of us up. I hope I did not create too much of the scene." Mildred expressed, dumbfounded.

"Well, at least it wasn't my imagination. I was absolutely not talking out loud, and there was no hypnosis involved. I must have subliminally transferred my thoughts to you. Explain exactly what happened to you from the first kiss to the final orgasm," KK said.

Mildred explained in complete and graphic detail from the very beginning to the final orgasm, and it matched exactly the fantasy that KK had been projecting. They were both amazed at the exact agreement between the fantasy and the dream.

"This is fascinating. Do you think I would be able to induce the same thoughts to you, if you were willing?" asked Mildred.

"I'm not only willing, I think that it is an absolute must. This certainly is of tremendous scientific interest to me. I would like to see firsthand if it does do what we think is happening. I'm certain that I did not hypnotise you. I'm also certain that I was not talking out loud, but only thinking. It is interesting. I don't think it was you, but I can't say to whom I was making love. I only fantasised the events."

They motioned for Megan to bring another round of drinks, which she did.

"You guys are certainly having an interesting scientific experiment in here," laughed Megan. "Mildred, you and I absolutely have to discuss this later on."

"There is really nothing to discuss," said Mildred with a sly wink to Megan.

"You actually did feel that?" asked a still astonished KK.

"I find it difficult to believe, but there is absolutely no doubt that it did happen," replied Mildred.

They spent the next half hour in small talk still centred around sexual satisfaction as they finished their drinks. KK settled back into his chair, closed his eyes, and held Mildred's hand while she continued to talk in general terms of anonymous people, places, and various sexual exploits.

KK soon drifted into a light sleep. Mildred continued to talk until she was sure that he was asleep. She then closed her eyes and began to fantasise the gradual but complete seduction of KK. She visualised him removing all of his clothes and lying comfortably in bed while she soothed and caressed his body. She worked her way down across his chest, caressing the soft hair. She moved sensually downward over his abdomen. She visualised his firm erection as she caressed and stimulated the organ. She moved her face down to the dark hair of his pubis, nuzzling and kissing. She then took his organ full into her mouth and began to stroke, one hand gently caressing his testicles. She could feel his orgasm building as his muscles tensed and his breathing increased rapidly.

KK exploded with multiple satisfying bursts it into her mouth, crying out in delight. Just as before, this outburst awakened both of them, KK obviously breathing heavily. The results of the stimulation clearly showed, as evidenced by the large wet stain that had appeared on the front of his tan trousers.

Mildred looked at him, KK looked down, and they both burst out laughing.

"At least I didn't make a mess," said Mildred. "Or one that is noticeable."

"How am I going to explain this?" asked an embarrassed KK.

"Perhaps a scientific experiment gone awry?" suggested Mildred with a wide grin.

Mildred and KK left the cigar room laughing. KK paid the bar tab, and they soon went their separate ways.

Megan looked at John. "Did you see the front of KK's pants?"

"I sure did. There was no covering that up," said Big John. "I think KK finally met his match!"

Conclusion

Some people, including reputable psychiatrists, think that subliminal thought transfer between individuals is possible. This has been documented with twins and people who are very close to each other. This can also follow posthypnotic suggestion. The common thread seems to be that the recipient of the thoughts must be willing to accept the mental transfer; it cannot be forced upon them. Thought transfer is often enhanced if both individuals have discussed the subject and are willing to participate.

The ability of the human mind to control many bodily functions is something we all experience on a daily basis. Consciously, very few people can actually induce an orgasm without sexual stimulation, but while asleep, it is possible. Almost everyone at one time or another has experienced a wet dream. Women are more likely to dream of sexual encounters and actually experience an orgasm in their sleep.

This was the case with KK and Mildred. They were each very much aware of what was going to be the subject of the thought process. Was this hypnosis? Was this posthypnotic suggestion or truly subliminal thought transfer?

Questions

1) Does KK abuse his doctor-patient privilege by having sex with these women? Technically they are not his patients, but he has told them he is a psychiatrist.
2) What is your reaction to his technique of convincing women to have sex with him?
3) Do you believe that KK truly thinks that he is benefiting or helping these women with whom he has sex? Is he delusional?
4) Have you ever encountered a true "charmer" like KK? Would you be taken in by his smooth talk?
5) Do you believe that subliminal thought transfer can actually happen? Have you ever experienced a thought or feeling that came upon you and you could not explain, but it was so real at the time?
6) Have you ever experienced an orgasm as the result of a dream?
7) Did you know that some sex therapists offer one-on-one teaching lessons?
8) Were you aware that men are seldom open about matters of sexual dysfunction, preferring to either ignore their problems or blame it on their spouses?
9) Have you ever considered straying outside of your marital constraints?

CHAPTER 14

THE SPARTACUS CHALLENGE

Geoffrey Kuban had worked for the local Portland newspaper for over twenty years. He'd started as a newsboy in the copy room, and he was now the chief sports editor. He was chief of three people: himself, a copy boy, and Lucille, a forty-something bundle of energy who knew all the facts about every sporting event that ever was. Geoffrey covered the stories, but Lucille was usually the first to know about a good headline maker. They were a good team.

Lucille approached Geoffrey's desk. "Here is something you might want to take a look at. This could possibly develop into an interesting story because these events have now begun to show up nationwide." She handed him an e-mail.

Geoffrey scanned the e-mail outlining an event called the Spartacus Challenge, loosely based on a TV series but being sponsored locally. The event started that day and would run through the weekend at the old Johnson farm in the hills west of Portland. "Doesn't sound too newsworthy, but on a slow Friday morning with a lull in the sports season, I'll go have a look," he replied.

Geoffrey always took his own pictures and had achieved national syndication of some of his coverage several times. He packed his Canon digital with a selection of lenses in his travel case and headed out the door.

He pulled his Ford 150 into the already filling makeshift parking lot that had been marked off just outside an entry gate. The Johnson farm was over one hundred acres of open fields, woods, streams, cliffs, and other natural obstacles. *A lot of people already here,* he thought. *This may turn out to be interesting.*

His press ID got him past the admission stand, and with a program in hand, he proceeded to look for areas of activity. Apparently, the Spartacus Challenge consisted of a series of obstacles that must be overcome by a mixed team of men and women competing against other teams as well as individually. The course and the obstacles seemed to be intimately connected with dirt and mud.

The course wound through the property for a combined distance of about five miles with man-made and natural obstacles strategically staged in many places. A fifty-foot cliff had to be scaled, and streams had to forded (always at the deepest part), with the course ending in a marsh area that had been turned into a mud bath with barrier walls maliciously placed. Entrants were judged individually and were also expected to complete the obstacles as a team.

Geoffrey spent the first two hours watching and photographing the contestants as they negotiated one major obstacle after another. He ended up at the conclusion of the course, the marsh. This was not just dirty but dangerous. Each team functioned as a tight-fitting group, helping each other negotiate the course. The sticky mess was made even more difficult by two ten-foot-high walls near the end of the course that had to be scaled, with contestants falling into the mud on the other side.

He was especially intrigued by one woman who appeared to be in her mid-thirties, but it was difficult to tell for sure. She was tall and in excellent physical condition, doing much better than the three men on her five-person team. It was apparent that she was the team leader.

She would make a good centrepiece for the story, he thought.

The contestants were helping their team members up and over the second wall at the conclusion of the obstacle course. They dropped into the mud on the final side and slogged their way to the finish line. Geoffrey identified her, still with a lot of mud in her hair, talking very animatedly with one of the referees.

"You know the rules of the course. You can obstruct but not physically confront any member of another team," he admonished her. "A member of the green team has accused you of kicking him in the face and pushing him back over the wall, which will cost your team fifty points."

"I did not push him! He had a hold on my ankle, his hand slipped on the mud, and he fell back," she screamed back at him. "He grabbed my ankle as I was on top of the wall. He would've pulled me over if I had not made him release his grip."

By now, members of both teams confronted the referee with their versions of the story. The referee realised that this was clearly a no-win situation. Because he had not witnessed the infraction, and without any solid evidence, he said, "OK, fifty-point penalty to both teams." Both teams backed down—any further argument would only result in more penalties.

Geoffrey had seen the entire episode, and furthermore he had good photographic proof of the green team player pulling on her ankle trying to dislodge her from the wall, and her viciously kicking him in the face until he released her. "That is one tough lady. I've got to get to know her better," Geoffrey thought.

She finished her confrontation with the referee, and she and her teammates took turns hosing some of the mud off of their bodies. Geoffrey approached her, camera in hand, taking some good shots of the cleaning process.

"Excuse me," he said. "I am Geoffrey Kuban, the sports editor for the local Portland newspaper. I would like to do a story on you and this contest. Would you mind if I ask you a few questions?" He extended his hand, and she shook his, mud and all. Geoffrey wiped his hands on his pants. "Would you mind if I get a few more pictures of you? How about a name to go with them?"

"Katherine Masters—Kat for short," she replied. "I live in Portland and have been doing the Spartacus Challenge for about three years. I tried out three years ago when it was just getting started, and was hooked after the first game. I love the challenge of each course; they're all different, and every game ends up differently."

"How often do you have a game?" inquired Geoffrey.

"It varies. They are all in warm weather, and we may do this every week or so, rotating sites so each team has the advantage of a home course. Our team trains out here at least a few days each week when we can schedule time away from our work. The challenge teams are more like a big club than an organized sports event. This is probably why you had never heard of us, we need more publicity."

"After what I've seen today publicity will be easily accomplished", said Geoffrey. "What sort of work do you do when you're not playing your challenge games"?

"I have an in-house day care for infants. I work out of my house, keeping small children under two years of age while their mothers work," Kat replied. "It is an eight to five job, five days a week, so when I am on one of these games, I have Sharon, a substitute, cover for me. Usually weekends are not a problem."

Kat was wearing a two-piece, skin-tight black sport suit, which was wet and practically see-through. Geoffrey took more pictures than he needed. The wet suit with nothing underneath it showed every curve and crevice of her tight, well-muscled body. She knew what he was doing and gave him every opportunity to get good angles for his shots.

"If you have time, I'm going to the shower trailer to clean up and change clothes. We could talk some more?"

"Take your time. I'm going to talk to some of the other participants," responded Geoffrey.

He managed to tag the green team leader whom Kat had kicked in the face. He introduced himself and asked if he could have an interview and take some pictures.

"Sure. My name is Edward Ashford. Our team is from Bangor," he volunteered.

"Is the confrontation I saw on the wall typical of this game?" inquired Geoffrey.

"That's what it's all about. Who wins is all that is important. We all play dirty and usually get away with it. That is part of the fun of the game. The risk and danger part is a turn-on for all of us. Kat is one tough competitor, and I have fouled her more than once. It's all in the game. No hard feelings—it's just how we play."

"What do you do in real life, when you're not playing these games?" asked Geoffrey.

"I'm an assistant to the state treasurer—pretty dull. This game is acting out a fantasy, and it is just as real as life for all of us who participate," Edward responded.

Geoffrey talked to him for a few more minutes and took some more pictures. Then he moved on to question some of the other contestants. *This has actually turned out to be an excellent opportunity. Good photo ops, great interviews, and a really interesting storyline,* he thought.

Kat came out of the shower trailer, her short dark hair washed. She wore sneakers, khaki pants, and a light blue polo T-shirt—still with no bra. *She really has a great body,* he thought. *And I would be willing to bet she knows how to use it.*

"What time do you have to get home?" Geoffrey inquired. "Interested in something to eat after that strenuous workout?"

"Sure. I can meet you somewhere downtown on my way home. Do you know where Dooley's is? They have great sandwiches," Kat volunteered.

"I know exactly where that is. I've known Big John for years. But of course, everybody in Portland knows Big John," Geoffrey replied. "Meet you there shortly."

It was seven o'clock on a Friday night, and Dooley's was packed. Kat had beaten Geoffrey there and secured two stools for them at the end of the bar. A Guinness apiece magically appeared, and they were soon into discussing each other's life stories.

Geoffrey learned that she was thirty-one years old and had two children: a girl, and a son. Her husband, Clyde was considerably older than her and was a CPA at Meyer and Barrister, a big accounting firm in town, and he hated her new sport. He complained bitterly every time she was out of town for a game, or even if the game was in town. He was very jealous and very possessive.

"Will he complain if you're late getting home tonight?" Geoffrey asked.

"He will definitely bitch about it, but that is nothing new. Many times the team goes out to eat at Dooley's or one of the other bars in town after the first day," she explained.

"I have never known a woman quite like you, and I would like to follow some more games, if you don't mind."

"Not at all. It would be great to get some good press coverage of our games. It should help attendance. These games cost a lot to put on, and the landowner gets a big cut of the gate."

"I think this will be a lot of fun and make a great story," Geoffrey explained. "I like a strong, dominant woman, and you will make a great centrepiece for this series."

Kat put her hand on his arm. "I have a softer side that you might like to get to know better. I need to get home before Clyde is totally bent out of shape. I texted him and told him I would be late, but he really hates to have to fix his own dinner. I will have to come up with something for him to eat when I get home. If I know I will be gone for a long time, I usually have something he can warm up, but I wasn't planning on this meeting this evening. I really have enjoyed being with you. How about tomorrow night after the game? I can fix Clyde some dinner, and we can stay out later."

Saturday morning, Geoffrey was at the course when the event started. He followed one of the other teams so that the story would not be too slanted, but reports in local papers always favoured the home team. This was especially true now that he had Kat, a local lead female, to anchor the theme of the story.

The day went well, and Kat and her team were well on the way towards taking the match early on. They ultimately did so.

Geoffrey suggested that they go by his house for burgers on the grill, explaining that his son was gone for the weekend. Kat readily agreed to meet him there after the game was over.

Geoffrey's home was in an older part of town, built in the late 1960s. It was a typical bachelor's pad, semi-tidy but showing a total lack of a woman's touch for many years. Geoffrey and Sandra had gotten married just out of high school. She'd walked out on him fifteen years ago with no explanation, leaving him with his son, who was now twenty-two and still living with him.

Kat arrived promptly at 6.30 dressed in her khaki pants with a loose green shirt over a white tank top. *Still no bra,* thought Geoffrey. *She probably doesn't even own one.*

Geoffrey offered her a cold beer and a quick tour of the house, and then they retired to the back patio where the grill was heating. A plate of six hamburgers rested on the table. Geoffrey set the beer cooler by the table and put the six hamburgers on the grill, and they took a seat on the recliner, taking in the warm, late-afternoon sunshine.

They sat and made small talk about the day's games. The west-facing patio combined with the heat from the grill prompted Kat to take off her shirt. She hung it on the back of her chair. Kat had small, firm breasts that were not concealed at all in the white tank top. Geoffrey could not resist the view, and Kat make sure he had ample opportunity for observation.

"How long have you lived alone?" she asked.

"Sandra walked out fifteen years ago, leaving me with a seven-year-old son to raise. I never heard from her again. She just said she needed to find herself, whatever that meant. I had to get our marriage annulled on the grounds of abandonment, because she never made contact with me again. Short answer," explained Geoffrey.

"I may as well be divorced," said Kat. "Clyde is so into himself and his work that he never pays any attention to me at all. The last time we had sex—notice I did not say "made love"—I seduced him, and he told me to never do that again after we were done. He said that sex is the man's prerogative, and I would be well to remember that. That was when I decided to do whatever I wanted to do. He is content to have a housekeeper, not a wife."

Geoffrey blurted out, "You could seduce me anytime you want to—and being seduced by a strong woman has always been my fantasy."

Kat smiled at him. "That could happen any time." She opened the lid on the grill, deftly slipped two burgers onto buns, and put the rest aside on the plate. "Leftovers? I do the same thing. If I'm going to go to all the trouble to cook something, I always want some left over for the next day." She paused and went back to his last comment. "I hope you're not thinking S-M with whips and chains."

Geoffrey replied, "No, nothing that drastic. I would just like to be taken. I guess that is the best term for it."

"Taken?" she mused. "Taken as in seduction?" She took a big bite of her hamburger and chewed it sensually.

"I guess that is what I really want. Seduction with enthusiasm—that would be a real turn-on. I must admit that the first time I saw you, that thought crossed my mind. The day I watched you giving that referee pure hell after you had just kicked the green team leader in the face, I got a hard-on watching you. I got some great pictures of you that day. Seeing you wet and sweaty and covered in mud in that skin-tight suit that showed everything that you had.... I would've laid down in the mud and made love to you right there," answered Geoffrey.

"That sounds pretty drastic, but definitely to the point. I am pretty certain that would have gotten me disqualified. Some weekday when no one else is around, we could go out to the farm and train for a few hours, if you would like," Kat suggested as she took another bite and washed it down with half a can of beer.

"Maybe we could do some training tonight," Geoffrey suggested. "How much time do you have?"

"Enough time to wear your skinny ass out." Kat laughed as she finished the burger and killed the last of the beer. "Where is your bedroom? We have some homework to do."

It took no time to dispose of what few clothes Kat was wearing; she never seemed to wear underwear or bra. She threw her remaining clothes on the bedside chair and pulled Geoffrey to her in a deep, powerful kiss. She pulled off his shirt and jerked down his pants; he too was wearing no underwear. She roughly pushed him onto the bed, climbed on top of him, and pressed her right knee into his chest, her steamy pelvis just inches from his face.

"What do you really want to do?" Kat taunted. She moved closer to his face, her black pubic hair barely rubbing his lips. "Want to taste it? Want to lick it? I bet you would like to fuck it, wouldn't you?" she continued in a low and seductive voice.

Geoffrey, still pinned down by her knee, could not move. She allowed only a quick flick of his tongue, and then she moved back. Geoffrey was absolutely wild with desire. He thought his erection was going to explode; still she teased and taunted him. She reached back and gently stroked his erect penis just a few strokes.

"What do you want to do, Geoffrey? Want to fuck me? Want to suck my pussy? Do you want it really bad? Not yet. I don't think I'm quite ready," she taunted.

Because her knee was still firmly planted in his chest, he was unable to move. His eyes were wild with desire. His mouth was eager to taste the fruit only millimetres away but forbidden. Geoffrey thought, *This is the ultimate paradox—desire beyond reason and yet the erotic torture of restraint to act on that desire. This woman is the absolute perfection of sensual manipulation.*

"How bad do you want me, Geoffrey? Beg me for it. Say you want to fuck me."

"Yes, my God, yes. I want to fuck you. I have to fuck you. My dick will explode if I don't fuck you. I've got to have you. Please, please."

"Not just yet. I'm not really ready. Are you ready now?" She started stroking his organ again. "I can wait all day. Can you?"

"No, I can't wait! I'm begging you, just let me taste you!"

Kat could no longer resist and pressed her vulva into his face. He devoured her, pulling as much of her into his mouth as he could. She instantly achieved orgasm, and amazingly enough, so did Geoffrey without any intimate physical contact.

Kat lay beside him. "Oh, my God, Geoffrey, that was erotic intensity beyond description. I have no idea why or how we did that. I have never possessed a man that way. You have released a level of sensuality in me that I never knew existed."

They could not stay apart for the next few weeks. She would come to his home, but more often he would go to hers. Babies will sleep through almost anything, and she did not have to get Sharon to cover for her. Geoffrey would usually park a block or two away on different streets, and he'd walk to either her front or back door. On days when Clyde was home, Geoffrey would go grocery shopping using her shopping list, giving her an opportunity to spend at least an hour at his house and then go home with the groceries he had bought as an excuse for being gone. Their games became more creative but always ended with the submission and seduction of Geoffrey to the complete satisfaction of them both.

They were in constant fear of being discovered. As little as Clyde loved or cared for her, she was his possession, and he guarded her very jealously, questioning her every absence. When they were at her house, they always had a number of escape options planned out.

It was Wednesday morning, and Geoffrey had finished his articles for tomorrow's paper. Not much happened midweek, and so the stories were short.

"Lucille, I'm going to the gym to start doing some workouts," he explained as he picked up an old, beat-up gym bag and headed for the door.

Lucille gave him a suspicious look. "The gym? This is something new, but you *are* getting a little full in the gut. Just don't overdo it."

At 10 a.m. he pulled into the deserted parking area at the Johnson farm and parked near the shower trailer. A few minutes later, Kat pulled in and got out of her car. She was dressed only in her skin-tight athletic suit and running shoes. Geoffrey had changed in his car into his gym shorts, a T-shirt, and old tennis shoes.

"OK, macho man, I know what you can do in the bedroom. Now let's try it in the field." She took off at a slow lope down the trail into the woods.

For the first quarter mile, Geoffrey was able to keep up with her, but she eventually outpaced him. Kat stayed just far enough ahead to be tantalising as he watched her tight butt moving rhythmically in her athletic suit. All he could think of was watching that smooth, repetitive, sensual motion.

They soon came to the deep water crossing, which almost did him in. The water was cold, and in the middle of the stream it was over his head. He was floundering and trying to get to the beach. Kat grabbed him by the back of his shirt, dragged him to shore, and unceremoniously tossed him down on the sand. "You wimpy piece of shit. You can't even swim, and you expect to fuck me?" she roughly addressed him. She grabbed the front of his T-shirt, ripped it completely off of him, and slammed him back down on the sand. While standing straddled across him, she raised the top of her two-piece suit, her wet breasts glistening in the warm morning sun. She turned and roughly jerked his shorts down around his knees, exposing his already erect organ. The fantasy was really working quite well.

She slipped out of one leg of her track suit bottom and straddled him, holding his arms stretched out. She began rubbing her pelvis across his abdomen. "Now, are you ready to fuck me? You really do want to fuck me, don't you? Your dick says you want to fuck me, but I don't think that I am ready just yet. I want you to beg me. Go on and say it!" she growled.

"Yes, yes, I want to fuck you right now. I have to! I will die right here on this sand pile if I don't," he pleaded.

"I'm still not quite ready." She continued to rub across him but did not allow penetration. Kat leaned farther over his chest, her breasts just inches from his mouth but not touching. "Do they look good to you? Do you want to taste them? They're hot and sweaty. What are you waiting for?

They are just how you like them." She continued to sway back and forth out of his reach. By now Geoffrey was wild with desire but forbidden to act. Kat was in full control, and he loved it.

Kat could not resist any longer. After releasing his arms, she slid down on him and let him enter her. They experienced an explosive release of pent-up desire in one massive, simultaneous orgasm that lasted for many moments. They rolled over on their backs in the sand, totally spent.

"Hi, Kat. You guys are really out early," a voice said.

Kat rose up on one elbow. "Good morning, Charlie. We decided to go for an early morning workout."

"Looks like it was really a good one. Don't get sand in your crotch—it's really uncomfortable." He laughed as he loped down the trail.

Geoffrey thought that he was going to die of embarrassment at that moment, but he was totally ignored. This was true even though he had interviewed Charlie last week at the games. "You guys certainly do have a strange culture," he remarked.

The games the following week were held in the small town of Killington, close to the Vermont border and a two-hour drive from Portland. The games were Friday and Saturday, meaning it would require a two-night stay in a motel. Geoffrey drove to Killington to cover the event. Kat went with two of her friends as usual. She was to share a room with Gail, her teammate. Gail was not married and probably a lesbian, although she and Kat had never discussed the subject. Kat explained to her that she had a friend who lived in Rutland, just a few miles away, and she would be spending time with her and her family. She was not sure whether Gail believed her, but Gail did not question her. Geoffrey had rented a room at a Hampton Inn for the Thursday and Friday nights in Rutland, hopefully far enough away that they wouldn't be noticed.

The first game lasted until 5 p.m., and Kat's team came in first. Charlie, the captain of the other Portland team, suggested that they meet at a local pub for dinner and drinks. Kat excused herself on the pretence of staying with her friend in Rutland. She was certain that Charlie did not buy this, especially after the encounter on the beach, but he said nothing directly.

"OK," he said. "Just don't wear your butt out tonight, or we will take you tomorrow." He gave a knowing glance at her.

Shit, I think everyone knows what I'm doing, she thought. *Certainly Charlie knows, but he would never tell.*

Kat had a cab take her the short distance to Rutland.

Geoffrey met her in the lobby, and they promptly went to the room. As soon as the door closed, he wanted to make love.

"No way, not now," she said, at the same time stripping off her sweaty clothes and stepping nude into the bathroom shower with Geoffrey following her. "Not now. I am tired, grouchy, and sweaty," she grumbled.

"I know you are, and I can't stand it. I love you that way. I want you," pleaded Geoffrey.

"No," she replied firmly. "This will be our first and possibly only chance to spend two nights together. We need to make it last."

She took a shower while Geoffrey moped in the bedroom. They went out for a good dinner at the best restaurant that he could find that served steak and seafood. This was the first time that they had dared to go out in public. *Slim to no chance of being spotted in here,* thought Geoffrey.

After a good steak and three glasses of wine each, they returned to the Hampton Inn. Kat gave Geoffrey a long, deep kiss. She drew back and slowly started taking off her clothes. Geoffrey matched her garment for garment until they were holding each other nude in the centre of the bedroom. Kat lay down on the bed, and Geoffrey followed her. He made no move, waiting for her to set the pace.

She rolled him over on his stomach, started at the nape of his neck, and nibbled and kissed her way all the way down to his buttocks. She rolled him back over and slowly and sensually licked his erect organ, thought never enough to get past the intense excitement phase.

Kat lay back on the bed and let Geoffrey explore her body, starting at the neck and progressing down across her flat firm abdomen. She stopped him at her hairline.

"You want to go farther down, don't you? You want to lick my pussy, don't you? You want to make me come, don't you? It is much too early for that. We have all night, and you can't go any farther down right now."

The anticipation drove Geoffrey absolutely wild. He wanted to possess her all over, but she allowed only a small piece at a time. She rolled him over on his back and straddled him, both knees holding his arms up where he could not touch her. She gradually moved her pelvis closer to his face, her pubic hair brushing his lips but no farther. She stopped moving and paused just in front of his face.

The musk of her damp femininity filled his nostrils. He wanted to have her, but she would not move. He struggled against her greater strength, to no avail. He could not move, and she was not moving. He was trapped.

"Please, Kat, please," he pleaded. "I want you so bad that I'm going to explode if you don't let me have you."

Kat could no longer resist. It was not from Geoffrey's pleading but from her own intense desire, and she pressed her wet pelvis into his face. After her first orgasm, she slid down his belly and let him enter her. She had two more orgasms in quick sequence, and as Geoffrey approached climax, she withdrew from him and rolled back over onto the bed.

"Not yet. We have all night. I don't want you totally worn out too soon. I can do this all night, but can you?" she taunted.

She moved his hand to her pelvis, and Geoffrey began to massage her until she reached another climax. Kat pulled him over on top of her and allowed him to enter her. She still controlled the pace of the movements. "Are you ready to come now?" She slowed down. "How about now?" She began to move faster. "Not yet." She stopped and pushed him off of her.

Geoffrey's testicles were now swollen and painful. "I can't stand much more of this," he pleaded. Kat pulled him back over on top of her and moved in sync with him. They climaxed simultaneously and fell asleep in each other's arms.

Friday night was even better, if that was possible.

Geoffrey was at Kat's house in the early afternoon. They had just started playing the "you can't have it" game when they heard the garage door open.

"Clyde must've come home in the middle of the day. Move, move!" hissed a remarkably calm Kat.

This was a moment that they both had dreaded but knew could happen. Geoffrey panicked, but Kat calmly handed him his clothes. "Get dressed in the living room. You can escape out the front door because Clyde will come in from the garage into the kitchen."

Geoffrey walked out of the front door as calmly as he could muster. Clyde opened the kitchen door and was greeted by a fully dressed Kat. Clyde was white as a sheet and obviously in some form of severe distress.

"Clyde, what's wrong? Are you sick?"

"I don't know. I felt really bad at work and thought I probably should go to the hospital, but then I felt better and decided to come home. Now I am much worse. My chest hurts, and I can't breathe," he said as he collapsed onto the floor.

Kat called 911. Clyde was unconscious but still had a good pulse and was breathing, so she did not start CPR. The ambulance was there within minutes and took him to Mercy Hospital. He had suffered an early but not fatal heart attack in a minor coronary artery.

Kat stayed with him day and night for the three days that he was in the hospital. Sharon watched her day care and took charge of the children.

Geoffrey stayed out of the way completely, unsure if there was anything he could or should do. Clyde's convalescence at home took over six weeks. Geoffrey and Kat met one time at his house on the pretence of grocery shopping. They could not bring themselves to have sex because the guilt of what they were doing overwhelmed them.

"Geoffrey, this is been unbelievably fabulous, but the mental stress is really too much for me. I honestly don't love Clyde, but at the same time, I married him, and we have two wonderful children that I love more than anything in the world. I don't know if what you and I are experiencing is love, but it's certainly the closest to that definition that I have ever known. If we were discovered, Clyde would be ruthless, and I would never see my children again. At one point, I found myself thinking if he died, we could be together forever, but he did not die. I'm sorry, but we need to stop now before this gets any worse. Some of my team members are already aware of us, and they would not talk, but someone somewhere eventually will."

Geoffrey did not take the breakup very well, as Kat had anticipated. However, he realised that he had no choice and she was absolutely correct. He continued to follow the Spartacus Challenge to its completion at the end of the summer. His coverage was so good that his byline was picked up and syndicated by a number of national media outlets. He did not try to re-establish their relationship, but he did stay in touch with Kat.

Eight months later, Clyde had second heart attack and died after a short stay in the coronary ICU. Kat and the children were at his bedside to the end. Geoffrey discreetly kept his distance until the mourning period had passed, knowing that they would eventually be able to get back together.

Conclusion

Infidelity is as old as sex and marriage. For countless reasons, couples grow so accustomed to the routine of marriage that they forget the fun and pleasure of each other's company. You cannot have infidelity without the loss of interest in the marriage and the opportunity for a new, exciting, and often dangerous liaison with another person. Infidelity is generally condemned by all major religions, but there are some societies where it is the norm.

Consensual infidelity is not necessarily acceptable, but it is passively approved by a spouse who for one reason or another does not want to participate in sexual activity. This person may encourage the active partner to seek relief or pleasure elsewhere.

Infidelity rarely ends well. When the deception is discovered, violence or divorce is usually the end result. In this case study, Kat wisely decided to terminate the relationship out of guilt and the fear of potentially losing her children, who meant more to her than her husband or even Geoffrey.

The other lesson in this chapter, in contrast to Latasha in chapter 12, relates to aggressive partners. Some men are attracted to aggressive women. Dominance, or at least an aggressive possession of him, is a sexual turn-on. Both Geoffrey and Kat found the qualities they sought in each other.

Questions

1) This story involves ordinary cheating for no other reason than discontent. How do you feel about Geoffrey's and Kat's behaviour?
2) How do you feel about the domination aspect of this relationship?
3) As a woman, have you ever been allowed to dominate your male partner? If not, would you like to? Would your partner be receptive to this idea?
4) Discuss the other possible outcomes of this relationship. What if Clyde's health had improved and he did not die? Where would that have left Kat and Geoffrey?
5) If your marriage had stagnated, would you consider accepting companionship outside of your marriage?

CHAPTER 15

SLEEPING TIGER

Today was Jenny McKinney's sixtieth birthday. She had purposely parked herself at the far end of the big bar in Dooley's. She didn't really want to see anybody today. She didn't want to talk to anybody today. *Just leave me alone in my misery and self-pity.*

Mildred, her best friend, had told her that if she did not get out more and mix with people, this was what would happen—and it did. *Of course, Mildred is not one to talk about mixing with people. I am one of the few people whom she sees socially Privately, however, is another matter.*

She had just finished her first Guinness and was deciding whether to have another when her thoughts were interrupted by Big John's booming voice. "Happy birthday, Jenny. We are not going to talk about how many, just congratulations on having another one. Drinks and dinner on the house for you tonight. I got in some great lobster this morning, and PJ has helped his mom clean them and put together a really good lobster roll, if you're interested."

"Thanks, John. You are truly one of my best friends. But how could you possibly know it was my birthday?"

"Oh, I have a way of finding these things out. You know how nosy I am." He laughed as he walked down the bar to serve another customer.

She was aware that while she'd been talking to John, another person had sat down beside her. She turned and saw that it was Mildred. "OK, so you're the person who ratted out on me to Big John about my birthday," she said as she feigned annoyance.

"Not a bad deal," said Mildred. "Free Guinness and a lobster roll. What more could you ask for?"

"Throw some satisfying sex in with that, and it would be a much better way to spend the big six-zero," Jenny replied. "I have spent more years than I can count listening to you telling me how good sex is, and I still can't make it happen."

Mildred thought a few moments. "I know we have discussed this before, but have you ever had any real satisfaction with any of the men in your life?"

"Two marriages and an occasional boyfriend, and I think that I might have accidentally experienced a sex-induced orgasm or two somewhere along the line."

"Your first husband, Miguel? Good-looking Puerto Rican guy was never able to satisfy you?" inquired Mildred.

"Mildred, you know more about me than most of my friends. But let me, in my current depressed state of mind, describe Miguel. Miguel knew that he was phenomenally good-looking, and he considered himself to be the ultimate stud. When I first met him, I thought that he was the sexiest creature I had ever seen. He was a very strict Catholic and said that he did not believe in sex outside of marriage, and so I married him. Really bad mistake," explained Jenny.

"On our wedding night, his friends had gotten him drunk, and when he finally came back to our room, the romance of my first time consisted of being thrown across the foot of the bed, mounted from behind, and my virginity shredded. In less than one minute, it was all over. And that was as good as it ever got. Miguel liked sex, but it was always on his terms—when and where, he always decided. Sex with Miguel was always fast and violent. He made it very clear early on that lovemaking was a man's choice. The woman's purpose was to have children—many of them.

"I had two children in two years, the second resulting in a retained placenta. I would've bled to death if my doctor had not done an emergency hysterectomy. Miguel never forgave me for this. He said that I had now become nothing more than an empty vessel, a worthless whore. Sometimes he would wake me up at night, beat me, and drag me to the edge of the bed, always having sex from behind. He continuously told me that I was completely worthless and served no purpose at all, and he was wasting good sperm on me."

Mildred listened to Jenny open up more than she ever had regarding Miguel. "He was Catholic. How did you finally get a divorce from him?"

"Because I was unable to produce the family that he wanted, he convinced his good friend, the parish priest, to interpret some vague papal law to have the marriage annulled on the basis of failure to properly carry out wifely duties. I was never sure how clear this was in the eyes of the church, but I didn't care. Legally, we did get divorce papers from the state, and I was free of him at last. He kept the children, and I was still able to see them, but eventually they drifted away," she explained tearfully.

Jenny picked at her lobster roll, offering some to Mildred, who took a big bite.

"John must have some real connection down at the wharf. I can never find lobster this tender," said Mildred.

They sat in silence for a few minutes. Jenny finally said, "Let's go sit at one of the tables and have another Guinness. Because you brought all of this up, I need your expert opinion."

They chose one of the back tables, Megan brought them two fresh Guinnesses, and Jenny opened up. "Miguel was a disaster, and Joe, my second husband, was just a dud—not his fault, that's just how he was. I honestly don't know why I married Joe, except there had been no one in my life for five years. I wanted not just the security of marriage but also a companion, which I had never experienced with Miguel. Joe was very nice, very considerate, and always a gentleman, but he was a total bedroom bomb out."

"Explain that one," Mildred prompted.

"The best way to describe Joe is that his idea of sex was ready, set, go, come, and go to sleep. He was not being unkind; he just simply didn't know any better. With my lack of experience, I didn't know any better either, but at least we had sex from the front. I always thought that there should be something more to it than that. As I said before, I think that I accidentally had a few orgasms with Joe, but only because I pushed harder and faster than he did. We were married for fifteen years. Joe was a heavy smoker and died of lung cancer five years ago. Now here I am alone, just two years away from becoming a virgin again. You remember the seven-year rule? I am approaching the end stage of life."

Mildred said, "That was probably just a little over-dramatized, I see your problem, but you are a long way from the end stage of life. Haven't you ever just, you know, played with yourself and had an orgasm?"

"Sure, I guess everybody does that. But it is just a mechanical thing for satisfaction. The few times I can remember an orgasm during sex, it seemed so much better."

"You've got that right," replied Mildred. She looked Jenny straight in the face. "Yes, you have had a shitty sex life, and your real life has not been a bed of roses either. Many people never do achieve satisfaction in marriage. They exist, and they stay with it because they think that there really is no other viable alternative. At sixty years old, you are not dead, just dormant and waiting for somebody to wake you up. You're good-looking, and you still have a good body; you've just got a beat-to-hell attitude. I know someone to whom I would like to introduce you. He is about your age and is a person who potentially could make a real change in your life. Quite frankly, he needs to be brought back to life too. The two of you might turn out to be a morose disaster, but I would bet not."

"Mildred, I am not in the slightest mood for blind dates, a fixer-up, one-night stand, or whatever else you might term this," stated Jenny with emphasis.

"How about matchmaking with Mildred.com?" Mildred replied with a laugh. "Seriously, the guy I would like to introduce you to is named Roland Barker. He is the sales manager at the local Mercedes dealer. He lost his wife four years ago. They were hit head-on by a drunk driver who crossed the centre line. She did not have on her seat belt and was ejected through the windshield. The heavy Mercedes 550 sedan saved his life, but he was never the same after that night. I run into Roland from time to time, and sometimes he is almost as down as you are tonight."

Jenny chuckled. "Now I see how you got such a good deal on that little red Mercedes convertible."

Mildred appeared to blush. "I have no idea what you're talking about." Then she laughed and took Jenny's hand. "Seriously, I would like you to meet Roland. I think you would really like him."

"OK, how do we go about this matchmaking venture?" asked Jenny.

"I will invite him for a drink at Dooley's next Friday night and introduce you to him as one of my closest friends who is lonely. Then we will see what happens," Mildred explained.

During Friday night and happy hour, Dooley's was generally a rowdy, packed house. Mildred met Jenny at the end of the bar at six o'clock. Roland showed up a few minutes later, and the three of them selected a table in the back. Megan brought the drinks to the table as Mildred formally introduced Roland and Jenny. At first conversation was a bit awkward, but Mildred quickly had everyone at ease with some of her stories about people she had known—all anonymous of course, but anyone from Portland could often guess some of the players.

After the second round of Guinness was finished, Mildred excused herself to go visit someone at the bar, leaving them alone.

Roland opened the conversation. "So Mildred tells me you have lived in Portland most of your life. What kind of work did you do during your career, or are you still working?"

"Short story: two husbands, one divorce very messy, and the second husband for fifteen years died five years ago of lung cancer. Two children grown and gone. I'm still working part-time as a legal secretary with Wiggins and Short. I have worked there my entire professional career. And you? Mildred tells me you work for Mercedes."

"Well, I don't actually work for Mercedes. I am the sales manager at Eskridge Mercedes here in Portland. I oversee the other salespeople and close the deals if needed. I've worked there for over twenty years. My wife died four years ago. We were hit head-on by a drunk driver. I survived; she did not." Roland almost broke down after explaining his loss.

"I'm so sorry," said Jenny. "I know what you're feeling. The loss of a long-time spouse is very hard to get over." As she talked, she took his hand.

Roland did not pull back but squeezed her hand in response. "It gets very lonely at night," he explained. "I'm very busy all day and don't have time to dwell on what-if, but nights are very long. I miss her, and I miss the companionship."

"I understand," said Jenny. "I also miss someone to talk to, to hold me and just be my friend. Do you see Mildred very often?"

"Mildred is a long-time friend, and someone I can talk to," explained

Roland. "I loved my wife very much, but Mildred was a true friend. I could open up to her. Not very many people are that way."

"I know what you mean," said Jenny. "Mildred and I have known each other for at least thirty years and have shared many deep, dark secrets. She thought you and I would be a good match, whatever that implies. But you know Mildred all too well to question her judgement."

Roland replied, "Same story she gave me. She must know something about both of us that we obviously don't know."

After three Guinnesses, Jenny blurted out, "She implied that it was a lack of complete sexual fulfilment on my part. Oh, shit—I didn't mean to say that." She blushed heavily.

This time, Roland laughed aloud. "God, that Mildred. Her entire life is about sexual fulfilment. That's also the same story she gave me."

Jenny continued, still blushing. "On the first date, I don't think we should broach the subject."

"How about on the second date, then? Next Friday?" asked Roland.

"That should be acceptable," said Jenny as she got up to leave.

"May I drive you home?"

"You really don't need to. I have a small apartment in McNulty Towers. I sold the house after Edward died, and this address is only two blocks to walk to work."

"OK, I will walk you home, then, if that is all right with you."

"That would be fine," she agreed.

They walked out into the brisk evening air. Roland took her arm, and she leaned against him as they walked to her apartment. Roland accompanied her into the lobby of McNulty Towers and was then uncertain as to what the next and final move of the evening should be.

Jenny pre-empted him and gave him a lingering kiss on the lips. Then she turned and said, "See you at Dooley's next Friday. Six o'clock, OK?"

"It's a date," replied Roland as he watched her walk to the elevator.

George, the evening security guard, looked up from behind his monitors and nodded at him. "Have a good evening, Mr Barker."

Roland thought, *George looks like he's never paying any attention, but he must know everybody who has ever walked into this building. I wonder if he could sell cars?*

At six o'clock at Dooley's, Jenny came through the front door. Roland was already waiting at the bar. As they were finishing their first Guinness, Roland said, "I have dinner reservations at Michael's at seven. If we walk slowly, we should get there on time."

"I love Michael's, although I don't get to eat there very often. It is very expensive, but the food is fabulous," said Jenny.

Roland paid the bar tab with a generous tip, and they left holding hands. "Damn, Mildred is good," Big John said to Megan.

"That she is, John. That she is," Megan said with a slap on John's broad backside.

The dining was perfect as expected. After a bottle of Silver Oak 2004 Cabernet, both of them were coming to a better understanding of each other's past problems and present feelings.

Michael came to the table after dinner, and he and Roland had a short conversation about a new Mercedes. "Dinner is on the house tonight," said Michael. "You haven't been in to have dinner in quite some time, and I haven't seen you this cheerful in ages."

"My life got a lot better since I met Jenny," explained Roland.

"That's great, "said Michael. "I will stop by the dealership next week, and we will talk about a new Mercedes as soon as the new models are available."

"Thank you, Michael. I'm sure that we can come up with a very satisfactory deal for you next year," said Roland as he left a generous tip on the table for the waiter.

They walked the two blocks back up the hill to the lot behind Dooley's, where Roland had left his car.

"The evening is still young," said Roland. "Care to come to my house for a nightcap?"

"We really haven't known each other very long. Would that be proper?" Jenny quipped with a grin.

"Well, we are not retro-aging, so I think we should make the best of what little time we have left," Roland said with a laugh.

Roland opened the door of the AGM-GT silver sports car, and Jenny glided into the plush leather interior. "It smells like a new car. I love that new leather smell," she said.

"It is basically new, with 1,850 miles on the odometer, never titled. The boss insists that I have a new car every year to impress the customers.

This car is a little too sporty for me. Next year I'm going to request a more sedate S series sedan," Roland explained.

"I sold my car. I don't even need one while living downtown, and parking is phenomenally expensive. If I go out of town, I rent a car. It's much easier." As Jenny rubbed her hand across the smooth leather, she exclaimed, "I have never ridden in a Mercedes. It sure is nicer than the economy sedan I rented last year when I drove to Boston."

They drove north out of town on US 1 and turned onto state Highway 88. Then they took the short road leading to the security gate of the luxurious, private enclave of elegant homes, Worthington Estates. "I think this is where Nedra Wiggins lives," Jenny said.

"Yes, Nedra does live here. For many years, she drove a Mercedes, but last year after she and Dr Furrer got married, she bought a Tesla. Said she needed something younger and more exciting than a big sedan," said Roland.

His home was tucked below the ridge line away from the ocean. The house was huge, on a large wooded lot with a circular drive and covered portico.

Roland helped her out of the car, and they stood there for a moment. Jenny took in the splendour of the entryway. "I know we are close to the ocean, but I can't hear it from here," she remarked.

"My wife hated the water but wanted to live here, so this was as far inland as we could build and still live in the area," Roland explained. "But we do have a great view out over the golf course."

Roland ushered her into the foyer and took her evening wrap. They were promptly greeted by very excited King Charles spaniel. "I want to introduce you to Winston. He never met a person he didn't love." After a quick rub behind the ears, he devotedly followed them into the living room. The room was accented by floor-to-ceiling glass windows looking out onto the golf course that divided the east and west sides of the development.

Jenny and her late husband Edward had both had good jobs, and so she was not exactly poor, but this was elegant beyond belief. She so expressed this thought to Roland.

"I like living here, but this place is more than I need for one person and a dog. Our children are grown and have moved out of the area, so

I see them only occasionally. It is just Winston and me and the weekly cleaning lady. You're the first visitor since my kids visited for two days last Christmas."

"I'm really glad you asked me to come to your home. I realise that it is difficult to let go and try to move on with your life. I have not done a very good job myself, but I am solely to blame," said Jenny with all seriousness.

"I have done the same. Work is easy; it always has been. Coming home to an empty house is not. Winston and I have long talks. and he is very understanding, but he really does not give any decent advice." Roland said with a smile.

Winston, who had been following them around, heard his name and woofed a response.

Jenny could not resist, and she got down on the floor to rub his ears and his belly. "I just love his soft ears," she said.

"Now you've done it. He won't leave you alone for the rest of the night. You've just made a friend for life. In fact, I think you have made two friends, or at least I hope so."

Jenny got up and gave Roland a soft kiss on the lips. "I hope we both have made good friends for life."

Roland gave Jenny a brief tour of the rest of the house, ending back in the living room with two glasses of Sandeman vintage 2010 port. They sat on the couch. Jason started the gas logs in the fireplace, and Winston promptly curled up on his rug, chin on his paws, keeping an eye on them.

"Jenny, you're the first person I have had an actual date with since my wife died four years ago. I just did not feel right about it. Maybe my friends are right. They keep telling me I need to move on, but where and how?"

"Maybe now is the right time for both of us," Jenny said as she set her glass on the table and took his hand. "Roland, this does not diminish the love you had for her; that can never be replaced. You can only hope that she would want you to go on with your life."

Roland put his glass on the table and took her other hand, but he said nothing as he looked past her and into the fire. Finally he brought his gaze back to her face, his eyes moist from holding back the tears. "You are right. Sitting here with you, talking to you, and holding your hands—you are right. This feels right." His hands moved up to her face, and he held her softly, looking into her eyes. "Jenny, we have only known each other for a few short days, but would you be offended if I kissed you?"

She said nothing but briefly pressed her lips to his. She then returned with more force. Roland responded, and they embraced in a long, deep kiss.

They slowly broke apart, Roland still cupping her face in his hands.

"Roland, I never had a man kiss me like that before." She pressed her open mouth against his one more time.

Roland's hands drifted down from her face to her breasts. Jenny did not resist and pushed her body against his. They sank back into the plush couch.

"Jenny, before we go any further, are you sure you're OK with this?" asked Roland with all sincerity.

"I am sure." She slowly unbuttoned her blouse.

"Then let's go someplace more comfortable than the living room couch and these big, open windows," said Roland.

They walked hand in hand into the bedroom. Roland accessed a touchscreen and closed the drapes, dimmed the lights, and turned on the fireplace. "May as well set the mood properly," he said.

Jenny excused herself. "I need to go freshen up a bit, if you don't mind." She walked into the master bath.

When she came back to the bedroom, Roland had retrieved the glasses and refilled them. He stood in front of the fireplace. Winston had now moved to his night time position on his bedroom rug and was watching very intently.

Jenny came up behind him and wrapped her arms around him. Roland turned handed her a glass of port. "To us, to tonight, and to whatever happens. No regrets."

"No regrets." She leaned up, and they kissed eagerly, yet tenderly. They took a long slow sip of the wine and set the glasses down on a small table by the fireplace.

Jenny had not re-buttoned her blouse, and Robert advanced his exploration of her breasts. She dropped her blouse to the floor and unfastened her bra, her ample breasts spilling out into Roland's hands. He leaned down and gently kissed each one. Gently and then with more vigour, Jenny could feel her pelvis getting warm and wet—a sensation she had rarely experienced before.

She unfastened Roland's shirt and dropped it to the floor. She sank her face into the soft gray hair on his chest, gently caressing his nipples.

They returned to another heavy kiss, and Jenny released her skirt and undid Roland's belt and zipper, allowing his pants to drop and revealing a solid erection pushing through his shorts. The rest of their clothes were quickly shed, and they stood holding each other totally nude. Roland led her to the bed and gently lay beside her. He began kissing her from the neck to the breasts and down to her soft belly, stopping at the pubic hair line.

He looked up at her. "Is this OK with you?" he asked.

"Honestly, Roland, I have no idea what to do now. This is beyond my experience level. So far, you're doing everything better than I have ever experienced in my sixty years. Just keep doing whatever seems right."

With no further encouragement needed, Roland advanced to her warm and now very wet pelvis. He moved his tongue into the cleft between the labial lips and pushed deep into her. Jenny felt a sensation that she had never experienced. A tingling sensation started in her thighs and spread to her pelvis, and suddenly she exploded into an orgasm far more intense than any that she had experienced before.

She cried out, and Roland again pushed hard against her. Immediately she experienced a second orgasm of equal intensity. He did not stop there, but pushed and explored with his open mouth against her vulva. She continued to cycle through repeated orgasms.

Finally she pushed him away. "Stop! I can't do that again," she said breathlessly. "What has happened to me? I have never experienced anything like that in my entire life!"

"My God, Jenny. I lost count. You must have had at least twenty orgasms in a row. I did not even know that that was possible!"

Jenny was still breathless, "That was more than I have experienced in my entire lifetime. What in the hell did you just do to me?"

Roland smiled at her. "I think I might just have awakened a sleeping tiger."

Jenny grinned at him, "Grr."

"OK, Tiger, let's see what else we can do." Roland slipped over on top of her and penetrated slowly, then moving deeper. Before he was completely inside of her, she again had a climax. With every few strokes he made, she cried out, arched her back, and had repeated orgasms.

Finally she held him firmly. "Please stop moving. Any more of those right now, and I will probably die the happiest and most satisfied woman in the world."

They lay still for what seemed a very long time as Roland's erection faded. He finally slipped out.

"With all of that, did you experience an orgasm?" Jenny asked.

"No. That is a little problem I have. It feels fantastic, but I have a lot of trouble finishing it off. I hate to confess this, but my wife would have one orgasm, and she was done for the night. She would often tell me that it was all right if I wanted to finish it off in the bathroom, but she was tired. I have never had an experience like we just had. I was so busy with you with that I forgot what I was doing."

"I hope nothing is wrong with me," Jenny said. "I just could not stop. I did not want to stop until everything got so sensitive I could not go on. Let's try again and see if you can make it."

"Let's try something different," said Roland. "You sit on top of me. That way you can control exactly what you're doing, and I will work on my end." His erection had returned.

"Like this?" she said as she straddled his pelvis and allowed him to penetrate deep into her. This move immediately released another orgasm as she leaned forward, placing pressure on her clitoris.

Jenny soon found the rhythm of pressing her pelvis against Roland, and she discovered that she could control the timing and intensity of each orgasm. Roland was pushing in concert with her, revelling in her repeated orgasms. He continued to concentrate on his own sensations and at last felt the surge and buildup to a fantastic conclusion. They fell back onto the bed, totally exhausted, and promptly went to sleep in each other's arms.

Many hours later, Winston's cold nose touched Roland's arm, and he awoke with a start. "You need to go out, don't you, boy? Sorry I forgot you." He got up, turned off the security alarm, and let Winston outside.

Jenny sat up in bed and went to the bathroom, and Roland soon followed her. Winston was back from his business, and Roland and Jenny lay back on the bed. "What time is it?" she asked.

"It's 4.30—much too early to get up," Roland replied.

"Too early for a rerun?" she asked.

"Never." He softly kissed her, advancing down to her breasts and across her abdomen. He had his hand placed against her warm, moist pudenta, his fingers exploring the depth of her introital cleft and finally penetrating her vagina. This took Jenny beyond control, and she immediately climaxed, repeating the sensation each time Roland removed and inserted his fingers. She screamed in delight, and Roland pressed on as she experienced multiple orgasms, each one blending into the next until she finally pushed his hand away.

"You have to stop. It is so sensitive that I don't think I can stand any more." She held his erect organ. "Is it all right if I kiss it? I've read about this, but I have never done this before."

"It is not just all right, it is a great idea," Roland said.

Jenny tentatively approached him, tasting the viscous, sweet liquid emanating from the opening. She took his erection full into her mouth. Roland lay back in complete ecstasy as Jenny explored her newfound item of interest.

This was completely new territory for both of them. Roland's wife had never even considered doing this, and Jenny had never had the opportunity or interest to do it. Both of her husbands were interested only in fast, conventional sex.

Jenny intuitively stroked his shaft in and out of her mouth. Each stroke brought Roland closer to climax. He had never experienced this level of stimulation, and with one final stroke, he exploded into an orgasm the likes of which he had never experienced before.

Jenny was startled at the force of the alkaline fluids projected into her mouth, but she loved the sensation. Most of all, she loved Roland's response.

"What do I do with all of this?" she asked, fluid dripping from her lips.

"Just kiss me, and we will decide then," replied Roland. They kissed and held each other in a long embrace, finally falling to sleep. "*Thank you Mildred*," they both thought silently.

Roland and Jenny repeated their intimate encounter many times during the next few months. They married six months from the day of their initial introduction.

Conclusion

The prostate gland releases a complex hormone following orgasm. This very effectively, although temporarily, cancels the desire for further sex. The endorphins released from the brain create a sensation of satisfaction. This combination is the primary cause of the male stopping and often going to sleep after sex.

Females do not have the "stop sex" hormone release, only the peaceful endorphins. Males reach a sexual plateau, usually within the first five to ten minutes, and are finished. Females often reach the plateau later, and although they could extend it for an hour or more, they may never reach an orgasm because the male is finished.

For reasons of physiology, Jenny was slow to reach the plateau and her first orgasm. She had never had a partner who realised the problem, and therefore she had no great expectations; she felt unfulfilled in sex.

Roland had almost the same problem. He was very slow to achieve orgasm due to decreased penile sensitivity. His wife was mono orgasmic—that is, one orgasm and she was done.

Roland and Jenny found each other almost by accident. Separately they were poorly matched to their partners. It was no fault of each, but this was simply how fate determined a match. Together they were perfect.

Questions

1) Were you surprised to learn that females can have extended periods of orgasms if properly stimulated?
2) Was it an eye-opener to realise that some females, under the proper conditions, could achieve fifty or more orgasms in a single sexual encounter?
3) Do you now understand why the male usually quits and is satisfied after he achieves an orgasm?
4) As a male, do you now realise why your partner is often not completely satisfied with the usual sex act?
5) Did you realise that there are many ways to lavish sexual satisfaction on either sex without true intercourse?

6) Do you understand the need for foreplay, the lead in to actual intercourse—the play period which brings both partners onto the plateau?
7) Jenny's first two husbands were diametrical opposites. Do you think it is possible to predict a man's behaviour before marriage without experimenting with premarital sex?
8) Is there truly an "acceptable" length of time between the death of a spouse and moving on to a new relationship?
9) What are your thoughts relating oral sex compared to conventional sex? Is the thought of oral sex repugnant to you, or is it a fantasy you would like to try?
10) If you have experimented with oral sex, do you find it more or less satisfying than conventional intercourse?

CHAPTER 16

THE MAGNIFICENT SEVEN PLUS ONE

To only our closest and most intimate friends:
You are invited to a select group, Eight Person Fuck Fest.
To be held New Year's Eve, 31 December 2016
Pre-party gathering at Dooley's, 6 p.m.
The real party starts at 8 p.m.
Drinks, heavy hors d'oeuvres, and bring your own party toys
At the home of James and Suzanne Rowe
1200 East Congress St.
Blake Field Apartments, Suite 916
RSVP 207-901-3000 by 1 December if you can come!

"So," said Suzanne as she handed the invitation to James, "think this will spark some interest amongst our friends?"

"I'll say one thing: it is definitely direct and to the point. You're a great social planner."

"I love to put a party together, and with the guest list we have selected, it should turn out to be a world-class fuck fest," she replied with a devilish grin as she grabbed the front of his pants. "Shauna and I put this list together. I don't think you have met some of them, and some will turn out to be a surprise to me."

They reviewed the guest list.

Suzanne Rowe, Portland, Maine
Shauna Stevens, Portland, Maine
Julie Barrett, Boston, Massachusetts
James Rowe, Portland, Maine
Richard Watson, Portland, Maine
Robert Markham, Atlanta, Georgia
Harvey Johns, Los Angeles, California
Renée Salva, Portland, Maine

"Four men, three women, and one ambivalent," Suzanne said with a laugh.

"Renée should count for two," said James. "She's a lot of fun."

"How about some basic house rules?" said Suzanne, handing James another list.

House Rules for Fuck Fest

1) Everyone at the party must have sex with every other individual at the party.
2) Girls must come early and often.
3) Guys should restrain until the finale.
4) Renée must follow the guy's rules.
5) Toys to be utilised at the discretion of the participants.

The day finally arrived. A light snow was falling, but the temperature was a relatively warm twenty-five with minimal wind—in short, a perfect winter evening. By a few minutes after six o'clock, everyone had arrived at Dooley's. They had the full use of the private back room to themselves until eight, when a large New Year's Eve party was scheduled. By then, Suzanne figured they would be well into the other, much better party at her house.

At 6.30, Ronnie and Larry, soon followed by Cheryl and Sherrill, showed up at Dooley's. James was the first to notice them standing at the bar, and he turned to Suzanne. "Add them to the party list?"

"Of course. The more people, the more fun. I just made up the title because it was catchy. Go ask them and see if they are doing anything this evening. After all that they have been through, they need a good party."

James went up to the four of them at the bar, and after showing them an invitation, there was an instant, unanimous vote: party, of course!

Big John had a copy of the invitation and shook his head. He handed it to Megan. "Am I just out of touch with the reality of today, or am I getting too old for this sort of thing?"

Megan replied, "That, John, is a group of totally uninhibited people who should be able to enjoy themselves as they see fit. Do you think the next party in that back room will end up any different?"

John rubbed her pregnant belly and patted her on the butt. "I will surely bet that we have as much or more fun than they will."

"We'd damn well better, or one of us is slipping badly."

PJ stuck his head around the corner. "Did somebody say were having a party?"

"PJ, we'll have our own quiet New Year's party later, OK?" explained Megan. "This party is only for adults."

"Darn. I never get to go to an adult party," grumbled PJ.

"Don't worry," said Big John. "Someday you will have more parties than you can handle. That I guarantee." Satisfied, PJ returned to the apartment.

After two rounds of drinks, the rowdy and randy group departed for James and Suzanne's condo. Once there, Suzanne checked the food and drinks supply, and then she paid and dismissed the caterers. She looked over the gathering—truly an eclectic and most interesting group of people. Some were truly exhibitionists who very early on would begin to shed clothing. Others were the shy and retiring type who would be the last to lose their clothes—but would probably end up being the wildest at the party. It was a remarkable trait in humans: those who were usually very inhibited about displaying sexuality often ended up quickly relaxing in the proper setting. This party was clearly going to be the proper setting.

Cheryl and Sherrill were the first to begin to lose clothing. The upper halves of their bodies were soon proudly displayed, quickly followed by Shauna, who was immediately rubbing her breasts against Cheryl.

"Those two are trying to decide whose are the largest." Sherrill feigned disgust. "Small, firm breasts are far superior to those big, floppy things." All of this started the beginning of a judging contest by the male participants.

Suzanne was too busy being the hostess to notice the intended progression of the party until she realised that Cheryl was clearly seducing Shauna on the couch while Renée aggressively pursued James.

Damn, thought Julie. *Aced out again.* She raised Cheryl's skirt to find no panties and proceeded to indulge herself in Cheryl's femininity. Couples and threesomes were drifting off into the two bedrooms as well as occupying some of the living area furniture.

Suzanne looked around and thought to herself, *This is going to require a major cleanup tomorrow.*

Cheryl moved on, and James was now playing with Larry, which left Shauna and Julie together with their clothes off for the first time in almost two years. They hesitantly embraced and then lost all inhibitions and plunged into a deep passionate kiss. "I really have missed holding you and loving you," said Julie. "Men are fun, but being with you was so different and so good."

Shauna breathlessly replied, "I have so missed the way you made love to me." She slid down into the seat of a convenient chair and spread her legs. Julie was soon on her knees on the floor, burying her face in Shauna's wet pelvis. It took only moments until Shauna screamed with the first orgasm of the evening, rating a rousing round of applause from the others who were less occupied.

Embarrassed, Shauna sat up. Everyone laughed, and Julie held her and kissed her again. "I had almost forgotten how good you are at that," Shauna said into her ear, giving it a playful nibble.

Richard was entertaining himself by alternating between Cheryl and Julie who, by this time had abandoned Shauna because she was interested in finding Dr Johns.

James abandoned Larry and found Sherrill unoccupied; he was soon thoroughly enjoying her pleasures. James was so busy with Sherrill that he failed to realise that Larry had come up behind him and was pressing a firm head against his still tight anal sphincter. Not missing a stroke with

Sherrill, he relaxed and allowed Larry to slip in. The explosion of pleasure was immense to be both the fuckee and fucker.

By 11.00, most of the attendees had fulfilled rule number one, often more than the required one time. People again separated into couples and small groups.

Shauna and Julie had both retrieved some of their clothing and were sitting on the couch in front of the big picture window, looking out on the snow gently falling across downtown Portland.

"I have really missed you," said Shauna.

"I missed being with you too. We used to have such great talks, and I always enjoyed working with you. I know we had that unspoken pact after that glorious night to not get that involved again, but I regretted not being back with you," lamented Julie.

Shauna thought about her answer for a few moments. "Is everything going OK for you in Boston? Are you seeing anybody?"

"Things are going well in Boston, and I like the work. The big city is exciting, and the social life is much more diverse. I recently met a real nice guy; he is a lawyer in one of the other big firms in town. We have been spending a lot of time together. The problem is that he is newly divorced with one child, and the usual custody and visitation battles are ongoing. I did not want to be a complicating factor in that, and so we are low-key, but maybe someday, who knows. And you?"

"I have been dating someone as regularly as can be done long distance. His name is Robert Markham. He is here at the party." Shauna indicated Robert talking to Suzanne. "So far we're just playing it day-to-day, but it's still a lot of fun. He is semi-retired, a widower, and working out of Atlanta. Fortunately, we can meet almost anywhere and frequently do. We were in Napa in October for the late wine harvest. It was absolutely beautiful, and we had a fantastic time. The biggest problem is that he's twenty-five years older than I am, and although right now that does not matter, later he thinks it could. I don't think the age difference is a problem, but Robert is still hesitant, worried about my long-term future."

Shauna paused for a moment. "Julie, that night you gave me something of unbelievable value, a wake-up call. I don't think that Robert and I would be where we are today without it. I shall always treasure what you did." The two women held hands and gently kissed.

"OK, you two, break it up and let a friend join you," said Robert as he came up behind them. He came around the couch, sat by Julie, and said, "Shauna has spoken of you in reverent terms as more than just a friend, as someone who became a very important part of her. All of this is a much clearer after watching you two tonight. That opening scene on the couch was fantastic."

Shauna reached across Julie and smacked him on the arm. "That was uncalled for! Julie and I were just getting reacquainted, and I did not intentionally want to create a scene. I just got a little loud. Julie and I have a bond and a pact that is paralleling, but does not supersede, your and my relationship. Julie and I are more than just friends, and you and I are even more than that, I hope."

Julie started to cry, and Shauna wrapped her arms around her and held her for a moment. "Oh, enough of the heavy stuff. The party was fantastic, and we are all great friends."

Julie continued to sniffle. "If Jason, my new friend in Boston, had not planned to spend the holidays with his family in Seattle, I would not have responded to Suzanne's invitation. I am so glad that I did come to this party. It has been great seeing everybody, and especially getting to be with you again. I'm happy to have met you, Robert, and I know you and Shauna are going to do very well together."

It's 11.30, thought Suzanne, *and the party has been an absolute success.* She noted that many of the revellers had coalesced into couples and groups, much as she had predicted. All of them were searching for their clothing and getting dressed.

Shauna stood beside her, totally dressed. "I don't mind taking my clothes off to have sex, but I feel much better being dressed when I am having a social conversation with friends." Robert was also dressed and stood there holding her hand.

Suzanne, never one to hold back, said, "You two look pretty serious. Is all this more than just a short romance?"

"We are thinking about where we're going next," said Shauna. "Robert is still worried about our age difference, but to me that means nothing. I feel for the first time in my life that I'm alive and in love." She kissed Robert passionately.

"Trust me," said Suzanne. "You two are going to be fine. Just follow your hearts; anything else is an artificial boundary established by others to keep people from being happy."

Sherrill was standing and talking to Renée, who was still topless. *A girl who likes to go both ways, and does so equally well, is good friends with a guy who can't make up his mind which way to go,* thought Suzanne as she went over to them. "Did you all enjoy the party?"

"This party would have been impossible to not enjoy," said Sherrill. "Best party I have been to in a long while." She laughed.

Dr Johns came out of the bedroom fully dressed, and he walked up to Julie and Suzanne. "Looks like I'm not the only one to be more formal."

Suzanne laughed."Sounds like that is the consensus of the evening. I have a few minutes to get the champagne out of the cooler. Anybody want to help? We should be dressed because it's going to be chilly out on the terrace in the snow, when we watch the fireworks at midnight."

Richard rescued Renée, who was standing by herself. He handed her top to her. "Do I have to get dressed?" she asked.

"I think it would be a good idea," said Richard. "We're going out on the terrace to watch the fireworks display, and it's still snowing."

"I want snow on my tits," said a defiant Renée.

"OK, I'm certainly not going to argue when a girl makes up her mind, but you're going to freeze them off."

"They won't freeze. They are the best silicone you can buy."

At 11.50, the doorbell rang. Suzanne could not think her party was causing so much disturbance that the desk would send somebody up. They also never called to say there were visitors on their way. "All very curious," she mulled as she opened the door.

Big John and Megan, accompanied by Dr Furrer and Nedra, greeted her with a magnum of champagne and big hugs.

"The party at the pub dispersed around eleven o'clock, and we did not want to miss the New Year's without seeing all of you. We knew exactly where to find you and figured you probably would be reasonably dressed by now," said John. "Nancy, the late-shift bartender, is with PJ, and they are going to watch the new year come in with the big fireworks display outside."

Suzanne said, "Come on in. We are going out on the terrace to watch the fireworks. I'm certain that you know everyone at the party, so no need for introductions." She escorted them into the room.

Ronnie and Larry were huddled in a corner of the terrace with Cheryl and Sherrill, wrapped in a large blanket. "Larry, stop poking me," said Sherrill.

"I'm not poking you," said Larry. "It's Ronnie. He's still having fun with his newfound toy."

They laughed and did a four-way kiss.

Cheryl said to Suzanne, "Thanks for letting us be part of this evening. The party was absolutely fantastic. It was great to be here on this special night with all of our friends."

Ronnie added, "Had it not been for the love and support of all of you, I would be dead. Now I'm more alive than I have ever been in my entire life." He kissed Sherrill. "No offense, Larry."

"None taken," Larry said as he embraced the other three.

Suzanne talked to John and Megan. "So how's the new kid in the oven going?"

John patted Megan's expanding belly. "We had an ultrasound this morning that told us that we are having a girl, so PJ will have a sister," said John proudly. Suzanne repeated the announcement loudly enough for everybody to hear, which resulted in another round of toasting and applause to the welcome news of a new member of the next generation.

John again raised his glass. "We must never forget one very special friend who is no longer with us. Let us drink a rousing toast to that one person, that one feisty old lady, who once she touched your life left you changed forever. Mildred, we all loved you, and we all miss you. She really would have liked this party."

Glasses were filled again with one minute to go. Suzanne toasted, "I want to thank all of you for coming tonight—yes, pun intended. It has been a great year, and we all have met new and wonderful friends. Most important, we have discovered and shared love, something many people miss for their entire lifetime." They toasted again to new friends, old friends, and departed ones.

The sky over downtown Portland lit up with a brilliant fireworks display. The primary ignitions were completely obscured by the snow, making a surreal scene with expanding waves of coloured light dispersed by the fine particles of snow. There was practically no sound due to the muffling effect of the falling snow, making the overall effect more of a dream sequence.

And so, as the often quoted saying goes, “Love triumphs all.” It was so true for the friends at Dooley’s. The lessons of love taught and learned through life should be shared with others. The sharing of your knowledge and skills could only make life and love better for all.

Conclusion

There will be those who feel that free for all sex is debasing of all the principles of love. In many ways, they may be correct. The conclusions reached in these sixteen episodes are not to be taken individually, but as a compilation of the knowledge of human sexuality and interplay between individuals. As stressed repeatedly, the act of sexual intercourse is only one component of true love. Love can be shared in many different ways with many different people. By nature, man is not monogamous. However, this monogamy can actually be strengthened by freely giving of ourselves to others but always returning to our original partner without shame or remorse. Sexual favours should not be indiscriminately dispensed, but should be held in the sanctity of a form of love and attraction between two individuals, actually strengthened by the willingness to share this love with others whom we also love.

Questions

1) What do you think of this party? Are there hazards here? Pleasures?
2) Can you see yourself participating in a Fuck Fest party?
3) Do you think this sort of party really happens anywhere? Hollywood? Communes? Your town?
4) Would you even consider participating in this type of the party if it were available?
5) Was this concluding chapter a fitting finale to this book?
6) What moral, medical, and personal issues did the characters in these stories have to resolve in their own minds before these stories could happen?

7) Does the age of each character affect the factors that each individual must consider? Are medical and moral issues different for people who are in their twenties, forties, and sixties?
8) In any relationship outside of marriage there are issues to consider: disease, pregnancy, emotional vulnerability, blackmail potential, professional reputation, obligation to others. Do you think these issues were handled properly in this collection of stories
9) What precautions did some of the people in the stories take to try to ensure their own safety?
10) If you found the activities of any of the stories distasteful and unacceptable to you, are you still able to accept the idea that such actions should be permitted for others?
11) Out of these sixteen stories, which one was your favorite?
12) Why did you choose this one as your favorite story?
13) Do you personally relate to your favorite story?

AUTHOR BIOGRAPHY

Roger C. Zocort, MD, is a professor and practicing physician at a major academic university teaching hospital. He carries an active practice of many patients under treatment as well as teaching residents and medical students. The material that is presented in this collection of short stories takes place around a fictional pub located in Portland, Maine.

The characters depicted in these stories are purely fiction and bear no resemblance to actual persons or places. However, the encounters between the characters, the graphic content of their revelations, and the circumstances of their relationships are inspired by actual case histories accumulated during many years of the author's practice as a clinical physician. Each of these case histories was the topic of student lecture material during teaching encounters.

At the encouragement of many of his peers, he was convinced that this information would be valuable to persons outside of the medical field. This collection of stories, and their associated messages and lessons to be learned, was documented. The case histories have been rewritten as narrative scenarios between two or more people. The reader will find that the clinical conclusion and the question-and-answer teaching commentaries following each of the stories will inspire a deeper insight into their own intimate relationships with others.

Dr Zocort has authored hundreds of scientific articles, books, book chapters, and lectures throughout his academic career. This is Dr Zocort's' first venture into a literary venue outside of the field of pure science, and it is written for non-professionals.

Roger C. Zocort, MD, is a pen name, but his rank, title, and teaching experience are quite real, as are the composite characters presented in this book.

Printed in the United States
By Bookmasters

Printed in the United States
By Bookmasters